Love Can't
Tell Time

Born in Phoenix, Arizona, Allison DuBois became aware of her ability to communicate with departed souls when she was six years old. After getting a BA in Political Science from Arizona State University, she worked as an intern at the district attorney's office in Phoenix. This got her interested in using her skills to help solve crimes. Allison now devotes her life to helping the living by connecting them with deceased loved ones. She's the inspiration for the hit TV series *Medium*, and a *New York Times* bestselling author.

Be sure to read her other books:

Don't Kiss Them Good-Bye

We Are Their Heaven

Secrets of the Monarch

Talk to Me

Into the Dark

Allison DuBois

Love Can't Tell Time

Why Love Never Dies

an Allison DuBois Book

Published by Lucky Maven Productions, LLC

Dedication

I would like to dedicate this book to all of the soulmates that I've reconnected over the last 20 years. Their stories have lifted me up and inspired me to value and appreciate all of the precious moments that I've had with my husband Joe and our three daughters. The wisdom and love shared with me from thousands of soulmates has become part of me and my life. The living tell me that they had one true love, and that's all they ever needed in their life; they will wait until they see them again. I find their completeness so beautiful. Soulmates are part of our souls, and we're part of theirs. Love Can't Tell Time is dedicated to all of the people throughout history and who've yet to be born who are lucky enough to be part of something so cosmically wondrous as the union of soulmates.

Contents

Foreword

I remember the very first moment I laid eyes on Allison. It looked as if a spotlight was shining on her, and no one else mattered. That was in the summer of 1992, and she was the most beautiful girl I had ever seen. We were married just over a year later. I knew nothing of love until I met her, she has taught me everything.

I cannot think of someone better qualified to write about love than my wife. She has all of the best qualities that you could hope for. Throughout our relationship, she has consistently shared her deep insights on love with me; she will think these insights are self-evident, and I will remind her that the rest of us are mere mortals. At the same time, some of her most extraordinary qualities, compassion and emotion, are ones we are all capable of, yet somehow she takes them to a higher level.

Allison was born with an ability to peer into people's souls and understand what makes them tick. She often knows more about a person than they know about themselves. How many of us can be objective while looking into the mirror? She has looked into my soul . . . and she still loves me. That, in itself, is a testament of true love.

When Allison was in college, she dreamed of being a lawyer. At that time, I didn't know that Allison had these unique gifts, I just thought she was going to make a damn good lawyer because she could see right through people! It has been a wild ride, and there have been many unexpected turns, yet in the end, Allison has done what she had always wanted to do, help people.

When I met her, it felt like I had found my other half. This doesn't mean that I don't learn new things about her all of the time. We are going through this life together, learning, having successes, and making mistakes. She is very inquisitive and intelligent. Even if another person exists that is able to read someone's soul, they may not be as interested in learning who people are. Allison has categorized and cataloged nearly everyone she has met. She remembers their energy and how it is unique or how it is not. My wife can access her memory like a phone book or a catalog of songs, picking out the energy to relate it to a new situation. Since she first and foremost remembers a person's spirit, she has an uncanny ability to do age progression and identify actors as adults whom we have only seen before as children.

With tens of thousands of readings under her belt, she has had the opportunity to sample nearly every circumstance imaginable.

I say nearly every because occasionally Allison will come to me and share a reading that is a standout, I know that people would not believe it. For example, Allison had a client who was searching for love. She wasn't sitting at home waiting for it, she was actively going to social events where the right people would be. It wasn't until she slowed down and went back home that she found love in her old neighborhood through a friend of a friend.

Allison is an ordained minister. For the people whom she has officiated their wedding, she takes the time to help them write vows. These vows are some of the most beautiful that have ever been written. They sum up a couple's love for one another and allow the attendants to peer into the deeper meaning of why these people need to be together. A snippet from one of the vows:

Groom: Amy is that woman who's the love that happens one time and lasts for a lifetime. She's exactly what I needed when I least expected it, and she makes me feel on an emotional level what I didn't know existed, and now I know what I've been missing. I feel like a hot teenager when Amy looks at me, but she makes me feel soulful too in such a deep place within me, there's such electricity between us we've been told you can see it.

Bride: With Bob beside me, there's nothing I fear because I know that our love will always save us. I can be in a ballroom full of people dressed up and celebrating, but if he's not there, then the room to me is very empty because he's all I need to feel alive, and nobody in the world has ever made me feel totally complete until now. This man has changed me for the better, and I look forward to seeing him every day for the rest of my life.

How can I be so lucky to not only have met Allison but to be married and get to spend my entire life with her?

Finally, perhaps the most important, and she will kill me for sharing this ... Allison is a hopeless romantic. My wife loves Valentine's day, she watches every romantic movie and cries every time *The Notebook* is on. Allison is lucky enough to live in a world where true love exists. She never imagined she would find it, but here I am!

Allison is a true expert in this field, and this book is a culmination of a lifetime of learning. In reading this book, I hope you get as great a reward of spiritual and emotional growth as I have in living life with my soul mate.

Joe DuBois
June 27, 2020
Scottsdale, Arizona

1

'Til Death Do Us Part, on second thought...

"I was always yours to have. You were always mine.
We have loved each other in and out of time."

- Maya Angelou

*H*olding on to love, even after death, deciding that your bond is so strong, you're not going to let your love story end. In other words, see you on the Otherside! Those who are lucky enough to have found their soul's counterpart and share a life with them, saying good-bye is unimaginable.

But, what if you didn't have to say good-bye? What if you and your soulmate could pick-up where you left off after you die? I can tell you that you can. I've seen it. True soulmates find each other, they're like magnets. The universe keeps throwing them together, and they're helplessly drawn to one another.

Your soul can sense your loved one's presence after they die. The sensation is similar to when you're immersed in your work, and your spouse walks into the room out of eyesight, but you *know* it's them. You know their energy, their vibe, their soul presence. Your soul senses its match. You don't need to see them to know they're standing right behind you. You can feel their presence. It's very much the same after they die, a feeling stirring inside you, telling you they're sitting on the corner of the bed or standing in front of you, even if your eyes can't confirm it. Your soul sees them.

When you see a bride and groom lovingly say to one another, " 'Til death do us part" it's both romantic and a contract. Committed couples who fulfill this contract of the heart, in death, will decide whether or not to extend their soul contract, to forever. Real love stories, the stuff that love songs and movies like *The Notebook* and *Titanic* make us crave, come from real couples. Couples who've managed to find each other and persevere through good times and bad. Some of them choose to continue their romance even after death.

When you're destined to meet, it will seem as if you two keep being drawn to the same place around the same time repeatedly until you finally connect. I can't speak for computer dating, but it seems to work for many people, and the computer could be the conduit that some people need to find each other. True love, no matter how you're brought together, your soul knows it's match. Your soul can sense when your soulmate enters a room. This feeling goes on after death, too. People always share stories of moments that they were sure their true love sent them a sign from the *great beyond*. I can often talk to their deceased loved one and validate the sign, but my clients don't need me to know who's responsible for getting their attention. When you get a sign from the love of your life, every fiber of your being knows it's them. Your soul and their soul have a deep, unbreakable connection, a bond, unlike any relationship you could ever have with anyone else in the world. When a partner dies, you might feel like you're alone on this planet, even when surrounded by others. Seven billion people can't replace "the one." Your soul becomes paralyzed, aching for it's match. The deceased feel the same way about you; they'll wait as long as it takes to be part of your world again. In reality, they're with you all night long. It's typical in a reading when I'm bringing through someone's true love the deceased will say; they like to lie next to and hold, the one who cries for them. They go on to say; it's because they held them all night long, that the living woke-up feeling a sensation as though the one they miss, was just there. They sense one other so strongly; it's as if the living could reach out and touch their mate or snatch them from their dream before they disappear.

<u>MY HERO</u>

ROBY AND JOHN

Roby

John used to say "we were made for one another—God just made me wait five days." He was five days older than I—48 years old at death. We had been classmates, then reconnected in college as friends, roommates, best friends, and then nearly 24 years of marriage. We were perfect partners; when we married, we became "Mr. & Mrs. Sweetie, Inc."

John had served his time in the Army before college. However, after the 9/11 terrorist attacks, he felt it was his duty to re-enlist in the Reserves, even though we had two young sons. John felt he had made a commitment to serve his country. After returning from Iraq in 2004-05 (as a convoy commander), he suffered from a few physical injuries as well as Post Traumatic Stress Disorder. His injuries caused him a great deal of pain and anxiety. Eventually, his pain and anxiety rendered him unable to work. With all that he'd been through, my husband made it his mission to take care of us, to help struggling soldiers and individuals, as much as possible.

Fast forward to finding out that my husband has cancer. His cancer advanced much quicker than we expected. We were partners; we were in this together, " 'Til death do us part."

In the last few hours of his life, while he was passing, he was unconscious. I knew he was trying to 'hang on' for his brother, who was on his way from Germany, and me. I knew I had to comfort him as much as possible, so he would not worry about us. I told him, if he needed to go, it was okay because, as I had always told him, we were partners. "No, you. No me. Just we." I told him I had some more work to do here, taking care of our kids, but that if he could wait until I was born, he could wait for me on the Otherside, too.

After he passed away, I was devastated and terrified. I felt guilty for not doing a better job managing his care and making decisions for him. I had no idea how I would finish raising and supporting our sons alone. I was bothered by the fact that he did not appear in my dreams. But, I sensed he might be around, communicating with me—or was I just crazy? Our song would come on the radio at emotionally perfect times. I would find little things, significant signs, I had not seen before.

I missed our time together. Our bathroom had been one of our few 'alone' rendezvous spots. (When you have kids, you do not have as many opportunities for private moments.) He would bring me coffee in the morning when I was getting ready for work. We would often share short, yet, essential conversations or words of endearment. We sometimes left each other notes or messages on our bathroom mirror, and for our anniversary a couple of years before, I wrote on his mirror, "I love you twice as much as yesterday, half as much as tomorrow! Sweetie, Inc." and the number of years we had been married. He left it, so for the next couple of years, I just changed the numbers. (It is still there, and I have changed the number twice!) After John's death, I put notes of strength and love around the edge of my mirror to help me get out of bed in the morning and get through each day. Examples of what I had written myself, had phrases like, "Team Hammer," "Strength," "I love you, Daddy" (a nickname for him).

"Help me!" "Breathe," and a close friend had added, "Daddy loves you . . . " One day, I was in the washroom having an emotional meltdown. Suddenly, that note came off the mirror, wafted out over my sink, and floated down to the floor landing in front of me. NOT STRAIGHT DOWN as if it had just fallen loose! I was skeptical and tried to recreate with air movement, etc. (even though everything had been perfectly still), but I could not make it happen. Was he trying to communicate with me? Was it a coincidence? I needed to know if he was still here.

When Allison read for me, almost exactly a year after John's death, I needed to know my husband was still there with me, watching over us, waiting for me. Allison told me that John had been "confused around the time of his death." This information fits with his last communication to me. He told Allison he heard me talking to him when he couldn't respond and felt me holding his hand. Allison relayed, I had "made the right decisions around his death," and John referred to me as his "rock," which is a term he had called me before he died, but no one else knew that. She talked about our boys, and almost everything matched up perfectly. She told me, he said, to "put his jacket in the closet" because "our clothes should be next to each other." What was funny was that I had an old sport coat hanging on the post of our bed, that had been there for a long time. Nobody would have known about it, not even my friends. She said he was with me and liked to touch my hair, tried to wipe my tears, and he knew how I would reach out for him at night.

I asked her if he had "messed with my mirror," and she told me he said, he "had to get my attention somehow." She said he played with music, my phone and moved things to get my attention. She told me our little dog (who was still refusing to sleep in *Dad's* spot on the bed) knew when he was around. She also said our youngest son (15), did too. My son later told me that sometimes he sees/feels a presence behind him when he is on the sofa (where his father often stood to cook or observe, when our son was playing games or watching television.) He said it doesn't make him uncomfortable; it is just confusing because it is more frequent when he is alone. Now, he feels comforted, knowing his father is watching over him.

Allison said my husband talked about both of our boys and is incredibly proud of them. Two weeks after his father's celebration of life, and on his 18th birthday, the oldest graduated high school as his school's Valedictorian. She said, he talked about how badly he feels, that our youngest son does not have his father to talk to, but is proud of how his son stands up for all his "female" friends. Both boys enjoyed hearing all of the things their father had to say about them, and, I think, took great comfort in knowing he's still part of their lives.

She also mentioned that John spent time with his brother in Germany, was with him, and trying to comfort him. She told me John said his brother was having a tough time. His brother had been unable to make it in time to say good-bye, but they were both very close and knew how they felt about one another. A few days after I spoke with Allison, I found a high school picture of his brother on a table on my husband's side of the bed. I did not remember ever seeing the picture, but I KNOW it had not been there a week before! Nobody would have come into my bedroom, certainly not anyone who would have had the picture or moved it. I contacted his brother, and (not knowing exactly how to address the topic long distance) I told him that I thought John had been thinking about him. I then told him about finding the picture. He admitted to me that he had been going through a rough time missing his brother.

Similar, uncanny experiences have continued to happen from time to time to the extent that even my close friends with whom I have shared stories find it hard, not to believe. I am now convinced, the perfect timing of songs on the radio and "phone dings" with no notifications are my husband, reminding me he is with me. He's still supporting me when I need him and giving me his input on various matters. I am so grateful to Allison for helping me to accept my Sweetie's presence in my life! It has now been almost two years since his death and one year since my reading. I continue to struggle, missing him dearly, but I feel a strong sense of knowing inside that I have work to do before the blessed day when I will be with my beautiful husband again! Knowing he is with me, wanting me to be as happy as possible, helps me make the most of my time with my amazing sons, beautiful family, friends, and students. I tell anyone who will listen, "Life is good! The key is to remind ourselves *why* as often as possible!" Someday, we will share his favorite spot on a sunny Caribbean beach, under palm trees, eating fresh oysters and drinking from a coconut! I am so lucky to have had nearly 25 years with my husband, and I got to create two perfect sons, with my soul mate. I've been blessed on so many levels.

MY TAKE ON ROBY'S READING

I have a soft spot for our military men and women. My dad's a Marine and my brother Michael was in the Army, both went into combat. I have brought so many of our heroes through over the years. Roby and John have two sons. I'm incredibly glad that Roby has two young men to remind her daily of her husband. It's a gift to see our soulmate, in the eyes of our children. People think that our brave men and women are only in danger while in combat, but truth be told, they often struggle with Post Traumatic Stress Disorder. It doesn't stop there; they also come in contact with harmful chemicals that can affect their health. I don't know if that happened with John, but quite a few first responders have died prematurely since 9/11. Due to the airborne chemicals, they were exposed to after the buildings came down. Soldiers are also exposed to dangerous elements in combat, and it affects them for the rest of their lives.

You can tell listening to Roby talk about John, that he was her world. They have a real love between them. John will continue to reach Roby through songs and "phone dings," letting her know that he's not gone. His passion for her lives on. It's easy to think that these are just stories, but they're more than that, they're someone's life.

When I wake up in the morning and look at my husband, Joe, I say to myself, "today, everything's good. Joe's here, and our girls are healthy and happy; today is a blessing." Because I know better than most, that life can change in a flash. One day, Joe or I won't be able to feel this happy and secure again. Unless we "die on the same day," as we've jokingly (but with fingers crossed) promised to do, one of us will have to say "good-bye for now."

The moments in life where everything is as it should be, are precious. It's a luxury to live your whole life without losing a spouse or a child. I see people who get that rare life, and I often deeply wonder if they even realize how fortunate they are to be whole.

Roby had 25 years with her soul mate; they built a life together. All of their memories intertwine with their souls wrapped up in them; they share a beautiful love story. Whether you're graced with 50 years of marriage or 5, recognize the significance of your togetherness. You've been blessed by everything kind in the universe. Some people don't get to find their great love in this lifetime. If you were lucky enough to be swept off your feet by someone who changed your life when they held your hand, I'm glad for you! If you didn't meet the stranger who changed your life this time around, trust me; you'll get another shot.

ONCE UPON A TIME

NICCI AND PETE

Nicci came to see me from Sydney, Australia. She was a bubbly, sweet woman, very down to earth and friendly. Past her smile and warm exterior, she held a deep sadness in her eyes. She wanted to hear from her husband Pete, and she had flown halfway around the world for this unorthodox 'date.' He came through, no problem. The pieces of their love story began to come together in the first few minutes of Nicci's reading and gave me a clear picture of the energy of their relationship.

Nicci

"Only the good die young" was always a relatively meaningless quote to me, until the day my hubby, Pete passed away. On that day, never a truer quote, had I heard.

Pete was and is the absolute love of my life. There is not a person around, who didn't love Pete. To know him was to love him. Pete's life was all about relationships; he truly treasured them all. He was one of those rare, unique souls. He was fun, cheeky, and playful. Yet, he also had a vulnerability about him that was so endearing.

It's safe to say I feel as if I've known Pete for a lifetime. We had packed so much loving and living into our lives. Our nearly 30 years together are worth a lifetime of memories to me.

We made one another whole, and we had two gorgeous kiddies (Australian for 'kids') together, they completed us. Our family of four loved fiercely and passionately. Each one of us knew just how much Pete loved us, and Pete knew just how much we adored him. Our love was our blessing to have amongst the hell we were living in, as we watched Pete deteriorate from ALS (Lou Gehrig's Disease). There was never an unspoken word amongst us. As time traveled on in Pete's battle with ALS, people had all sorts of advice for us, and the biggest was to say all the things you *needed* to say. It warmed my heart to know that there were no words left unsaid for us; we had been saying them for thirty years.

Despite the hideousness of this disease, despite the sadness and tragedy, the four of us managed to laugh a lot. Due in part to Pete's great attitude. It gave us the strength and power to see the days through. I learned very quickly that the true essence of a person is realized after a terminal diagnosis. What I saw with Pete blew me away. He never once asked "Why me?" despite having a life ahead of him to live, he was only 50 years old. We had two years to try and understand the devastation that is the savage beast of his disease. Pete did it with grace, humility, and with such a rarified dignity, even when there was none, to be had. He did it with a smile, a thumbs up for the kids, and a massive wink for me. In this precious man's body, there wasn't an angry bone, a true testament to what an incredible man he is.

I told the kids while delivering Pete's eulogy that he would have moved heaven and earth for them. Our plan is still the same for him to move heaven and, for me, to move the earth. That way we can meet somewhere in the middle.

During his illness and when he finally passed away, the kids and I were completely shattered, we still are. There is just no knowing how to put life back together again. How can I possibly live, survive, and parent without Pete? I don't know how to do life without him, nor do I want to.

And so began the search.

The search for what? I wasn't even sure. The quest to heal? The search to grasp at anything possible? I knew it was out of desperation, but the search had to continue, as it was the only thing giving me a purpose.

Amongst 100's of self-help and grief books that I was pouring over, I stumbled upon Allison's books. They spoke to my soul in a way nothing else had managed to do.

I knew I had to meet this incredible woman, and I knew it had to be in person. An over the phone reading just wouldn't cut it, for me. I knew that she would give me the one thing I had been longing for; she would bring me what I had thought was an impossibility. She would help me connect with Pete; of this, I had, no doubt. People thought I was mad, but something so strong inside of me compelled me to do this. I was steadfast in my decision, and nothing could sway me.

NICCI'S READING

Pete began our reading by saying that I was his best friend, "always was and always will be." He thanked me for his "beautiful life," and said it was "perfect," and he wouldn't change a thing. I felt like my heart had permission to beat again.

Allison explained that in heaven, souls always revert to an age when they were happiest on earth, reverting to a happy or vibrant time in their lives. Pete kept showing Allison the number 33 as the age that was his heaven on earth. It's fitting to know that he chose the age of 33, to go back to in spirit. That was when he and I were married, and we just had both our kids, our family was complete. This information meant so much to me.

Allison mentioned that Pete knew I was wearing both his and my wedding rings the day I saw her. I had flown over to the United States from Sydney, Australia, with our matching wedding bands, which I wore that day and didn't always wear together. Pete's was too big for me, and I was always worried that I would lose it. Pete said to "keep the rings together" that was important to him; apparently, he liked it that way.

Allison said, "whatever compelled you to bring and wear both wedding rings, was Pete communicating with you, and listening? The *urges* that we get, to do something for our deceased loved ones, are one of the ways the dead communicate with the living."

She said, "Pete wished he could take me on just one more date; it would be to the movies and dinner." No surprise to me, that was our all-time favorite night out.

He told her that all he wants is more time with me, and in his version of heaven, he is waiting to take me on this date and he will wait 50 years if need be.

He said he will always love me.

Allison was clearly touched, feeling how strongly, Pete loved me. She said we had a genuine love, and she could see how our hearts might even beat at the same pace.

The morning of my reading, while in my hotel getting ready, I said to myself that if I get a wink from Pete, I will know all I need to know.

He loved to wink at me, until his very last day when only his eyes could move, he winked at me. That spoke volumes to me when communication became almost impossible.

Sure enough, mid-reading, Allison chuckled and said, "He keeps winking at you."

My heart leaped, as I now knew for sure this was him!

He thanked me for the beautiful life I gave him, saying, if it weren't for me, he would have had an ordinary life and still died at 51. He was so grateful for his life.

To hear this is such a blessing, a true gift from the Otherside.

He said that he would marry me again and that one lifetime wasn't enough.

He asked me to "go another round with him."

He described to her the banter back and forth that we shared. The playful bickering was so uniquely us. He said it would "always end in a laugh or a smile."

No words could be more accurate; this description is US!

Pete told Allison that I still receive mail that is addressed to us both.

He said, some days, it makes me smile. Other days seeing his name on an envelope makes me cry. It's true.

He also knew that I had recently bought a new car.

He remarked how my new car totally "fits my personality."

Another fantastic spot on message: the kids always tell me how my new Mini-Cooper is so me!

He said that he loves to drive with me that I'm "his precious cargo." When Pete was sick, we spent a lot of time driving around, talking, and listening to music. Priceless moments together.

He said that he connects to me through music and that this would be no surprise to me.

My car basically runs on music and not petroleum.

He said that his song to me, a song that I will continually hear and know that's it's him, is "How Deep Is Your Love" by the Bee Gees. He said that song is his message to me. No surprise, I adore that song.

He described explicitly what I have done with our closet and where and how I have moved things. Facts that Allison could never possibly have known, descriptions that could have knocked me over with a feather.

He showed Allison how he would take the back of my hand, bring it up to his mouth and kiss the back of it.

This was Pete's signature move for me, it began very early on in our relationship and continues clearly, to this day. Precious information she could never have known.

He had such personal and tender messages for both the kids and I. This allowed our children to know that there was no mistaking the fact that this was "their dad."

More important than anything, Pete showed me that he is everywhere, wherever, the kids and I are. We are his heaven. He knows no sense of loss, as far as he's concerned, he is still my hubby, and will always be the boys' dad.

My job now is to learn how to communicate with him in a soulful way. I will pay attention over time, and with patience and practice, learn how to make our halves, whole again.

WHAT ALLISON'S READING MEANT TO ME:

After the reading, I was overwhelmed but felt that I had a lightness to my being that I had never felt before. To know that our love fit together so seamlessly blessed my heart.

Allison mentioned that she had been searching for a while to fill her last love story vacancy in one of her chapters and knew that we were a perfect fit after our reading. I traveled from Australia to the United States, with one purpose only, to meet with Allison and to talk to Pete. Connecting with Pete seemed easy for her, clearly showing our readiness and eagerness to be together again.

To try and articulate what Allison's reading meant to me, is very difficult. Words simply don't suffice. I saw the experience as more than a reading, more like a significant exchange, an exchange that allowed Pete and I, to revel in our love once again. It was like my love, and my soul found its way back to my darling Pete. What could be more special?

While Pete was sick, knowing the outcome of his illness, I used to say to him so many times, "Our love transcends this lifetime."

I said it to appease my husband's fear of us not being together forever, and probably my own. Allison allowed me to believe these words; she gave me every reason to know that these words, I say, are real. So, now I know that I can keep my promise to my beautiful hubby forever. Our love does transcend this lifetime.

My reading felt like a gift-wrapped present directly given to me from Pete; it's one I will treasure forever and keep locked away until the day I see him again. I thanked Allison for giving me a tiny piece of my heart back, she sticky taped my fractured soul back together, in some small way.

One of the MOST healing pieces of information, Allison shared with me was that, "Every day that I wake-up, I am one day closer to being with Pete. He is not my past; he is my present and my future. I'm moving towards him, not away, from the last day I saw him alive."

She said, "it's all about perspective," and what a beautiful perspective it is.

What was also calming to hear was that our departed want very much for us to live and be happy. For us all to make memories, as they will be along for the whole ride. To not feel guilty, for laughing and having fun, but rather smile, knowing they're standing right there, smiling back at you.

Allison and her gift are unique and truly exceptional. I could not in a million years be more grateful for my experience with her than I am.

TO PETE:

OUR LOVE IS A FOREVER LOVE AS WE PROMISED TO ONE ANOTHER ON THE 9TH OF MAY 1993! I LOVE YOU AS MUCH TODAY IF NOT MORE THAN THE FIRST DAY I CLAPPED EYES ON YOU. GO WELL, MY DARLING MAN. BE FREE OF THE CONSTRAINTS THAT THIS DISEASE BROUGHT YOU; IT NEVER DEFINED YOU. PETE, I'D CHOOSE YOU IN 100 LIFETIMES, IN A 100 WORLDS, IN ANY VERSION OF REALITY, I'D FIND YOU AND CHOOSE YOU.

MY TAKE ON NICCI'S READING

Nicci's husband, Pete, struck me to be a sincere, friendly, salt-of-the-earth guy. Easy to like, personable and his family meant everything to him. Pete came through in the reading, trying to joke around with Nicci, to get her to laugh. Not just because he wanted the moment to be "just like old times" but because he doesn't like to see his sweetheart sad. When spouses come through in a reading, it's often the "old times" that were the best moments of their lives. After all, those old times were fueled by love, the good times, and the bad; they rode it out together. Life is a grand construction job, you build a life together, and then you can't remember what life was like before you met, your soul mate. It feels as though your life started when you laid eyes on them, for the first time. Pete and Nicci had that synergy.

Pete's focus seemed to be on letting Nicci know that their life together wasn't long enough. He wanted more time with her, which he assured her they would have one day. He mentioned the names of relatives that he was around in spirit. Towards the end of Nicci's reading, it became clear to her why Pete mentioned those names. Sometimes, the living can miss seeing life through the eyes of our elders. Nicci's Aunt Edie wanted to be acknowledged in the reading. Nicci wasn't sure why she didn't think they were that close. Then, it dawned on her that she had visited Edie, the day before Edie died. Edie was just letting Nicci know that she was okay and appreciated the visit, in the last hours of her life. Edie "crashed" Pete's reading (he was OK with it), she saw it as a way to let her niece know that she matters to her; and, she'll be around!

After spending time listening to Pete talk about the people, he was around. He had messages for his kids and family. He told Nicci that his sign to her that he's around is the song "How Deep Is Your Love" by the Bee Gees. One of Nicci's favorites! He said he'd "marry her all over again" and that he loved the picture of him at work, to let his dad know. Watching Nicci's face brighten as she listened to Pete's words to her, was like watching someone's soul, wake-up! After her reading, we hugged, and my job was complete. The 6th step of the grieving process, "Reconnection" was achieved. Nicci and Pete were on the same energy page, making it easier for him to reach her directly and not have to work through other people. She sent me an email later saying that "You taped the pieces of my heart back together in some small way." People tell me they don't know how I can handle the intensity of bringing people through in readings. I say to them, "How can I NOT?"

Most fairytales finish with the words *The End;* real love stories don't come to an end. Nicci and Pete's story isn't over.

KINDRED SPIRITS

JESSICA AND VALERIE

Jessica

There are two certainties we are all bound to go through in this lifetime; being restrained by time and death. I would like to think of death as more like becoming free from our shells as ultimately, our souls shall forever live on, and with that comes all the love we take with us from our journey. Although time is part of us now, I'm a firm believer that the concept of "time" will eventually not be thought of in the afterlife. So let's face it, we should all live life to the fullest and love each other, every day, while we can.

People say that not everyone will live to find "their true love," As a matter of fact, I was once in that percentage of people who would always laugh and doubt the idea of a "soulmate." Until, I met Valerie at Primrose Retirement Communities in Mansfield, Ohio. Our special place, where we both found each other's hearts.

I'd like to start off saying that I am a firm believer in the thought that "everything happens for a reason." Even if we cannot fully understand why we go through some of the darkest battles throughout our journey in this life, I believe God never gives us more than we can handle. It wasn't until I was 30 years old that I finally got to meet my other half, and I am eternally grateful for that. I got the chance to know what 'love' truly means. Even if it was only for three and a half years, I am confident that our love continues and will carry us into the next realm that we long for as our home, heaven.

For me growing up, it was never easy finding a partner. A secret that I had held within me for many years was always a struggle until I met Valerie. August of 2015, was a time in my life that I would never forget as the year, I found not only my soulmate but my best friend. The most beautiful, red-haired, small-town girl, with gorgeous green eyes, from Shreveport, Louisiana! She moved to Ohio and was destined to eventually end up in Mansfield, where we met at Primrose Retirement Communities. An assisted living community that will forever be remembered as the

place, we both found each other. It was not very far into our relationship when Val informed me of a disturbing health concern
she needed to tell me about. She had known for a little over a
year and yet, never went to see a doctor. As a Nurse, I immediately insisted on figuring out the truth and that we did, even if it
meant finding the worst possible diagnosis at the age of 29. Who
was I kidding? I knew deep down that I was in it for the long
haul. I never saw myself walking away from her. I could never
walk away from the amazing girl I had fallen head over heels for,
the minute we laid eyes on one another.

On January 29, 2016, Valerie and I made the dreadful visit to
the doctor's office. Only to find out that she had been diagnosed
with stage 3 breast cancer. Was this happening to us? I will never
forget the fear I felt, and the terrified look on both of our faces.
Though deep down, we both knew it did not look good. We had
both felt a tumor on her right breast about the size of a golf ball.
To this day, I don't understand why Valerie took so long to find
out what was wrong with her. But, I guess it just comes down to
one's fear of the unknown, attempting to "kick the can down the
road," to be dealt with another day. Maybe Valerie could sense
that nothing would save her and better her to live freely, without
hearing the diagnosis? Who knows? I knew all we could do at
this point was to move forward. I can't say it was going to be
easy, not knowing how things were going to go. And even worse,
watching the person you love the most in the world go through so
much fear and pain.

Not once, but two times, within months. She was so young; it
wasn't fair. These were the most challenging moments of my life.
I was both her caregiver and her life partner at the same time.

There were endless doubts and questions as to why this was happening to a perfectly healthy 29-year-old young woman? She had no family history of breast cancer and no risk factors. It just didn't make any sense. I've concluded that we are all destined our own path in life, and without a good background of faith, we are left with questions and anger. I am a firm believer in God's plan for each one of us.

Without being graced by this beautiful girl, I probably would have never had the strength and will to have come out to the world. Not to mention sharing with you all our unique love and the connection we both shared. Three years is a short time for most people, but those few years were everything to us. People always said we shared a bond and chemistry that only old married couples share. I would have to agree with them, not to mention the memories we built and collected in little shoe boxes, along with numerous videos sent to each other on our cell phones. Those are the memories that I will forever cherish and have to look back on. How long you're married doesn't necessarily mean there was more love there, just more opportunities to appreciate one another. Many married couples grow apart. We had solidarity up until we whispered, our last 'I love you.'

It's been almost a year since Val's passing, and not a day goes by, that I don't think about her and everything she taught me, along the way. She always said, "just be yourself and live life without any regrets." Most importantly, I learned that regardless of her biggest fear, her fear of dying, it did not stop her from looking cancer straight in the eye and living and loving with reckless abandon. She once said to me in a letter, "Jess, if cancer takes my life, it is okay, because ultimately I'm fighting to live for us. I am doing all of this for a future together, but if things end up going wrong, I want you always to remember that I loved you with my whole heart. My intention was never to get you to fall in love with me and for this to happen to us. Just look at our pictures. Look at your ring and know, I still love you, from the Otherside. If possible, I will try to guide you from that side, checking in on you daily. I will kiss you on the cheek as you sleep and be that voice telling you not to drink your sorrows away. Instead, look through our pictures, read our letters to each other, listen to our favorite songs, and know that I'll still be there sitting next to you, loving you forever."

After going through my significant loss, I feel that I have grown so much in learning about my spirituality and where I go from here. Shouldn't we all be a little interested in life after death? As we have to be more than just a physical body. As I see it, we are each a soul, a spirit within our body living with a purpose.

For several months, I did my research on mediums and psychics and knowing the difference. I finally read about Allison DuBois on You-Tube. I have always been pretty open-minded in learning about extraordinary abilities, and as I see it, if God gives certain people gifts, why not use them to help others in healing? However, not everyone approves of communicating with the deceased. That's fine because at the end of the day, we all have our own opinions and views (which should be respected). However, in The Bible, under The New Testament, Jesus and his Disciples were doing similar things (praying and talking to/seeing spirits) all the time. I would see their experiences as acts of mediumship. Such as the story of the transfiguration where Moses and Elijah appear in front of Jesus and his Disciples. They reported witnessing this instance as if he was talking to dead people. Some people might say that it was Jesus, but according to the Gospel of John, it was noted that Jesus said, "All these works that I do, you shall do in greater works than these." He encouraged his Disciples to be open to these experiences. Also, the Apostle Paul noted these as the "gifts of the Spirit," which he details as a positive series of teaching moments that we would all have available to us.

On October 31, 2019, I had my reading with Allison in which I was not only convinced but was reassured with a sense of knowing, that my sweet angel girl Valerie was with me once again. It was undeniable; she had orchestrated this important date of ours for the reading. From the very beginning of the reading, she apologized through Allison in the same words; she'd always say to me while she was alive. She acknowledged her love for me in detail with specific places and events that had occurred within the last six months. I had gotten the memorial tattoo for her, the personal necklace that I wear every day; she was aware of all of it.

Most importantly, she recognized my need to move from Ohio. I had been debating back and forth on whether or not to move since her passing. I have realized that she is more alive now in spirit; she is still here now, living her version of heaven through us. After all, "we are their heaven." Our love has not ended; we have reached a new chapter 'til the day we reunite again. When Allison closed our reading, she stated in Valerie's words, as she always used to tell me, "Don't forget, I love you more." I could not have been happier to hear that at this moment in time.

After going through my reading, I could not have been more at ease knowing, Val was still present with me every day. Every day that goes by, I now see, as a day closer to reuniting with her. A day closer, as our love shall pick up where it had left off, a day closer to being together again, one day never to part.

MY TAKE ON JESSICA'S READING

Jessica's reading was full of messages. Her fiancee' Valerie came through strong and focused on what she wanted, no *needed* to say to Jessica. Valerie and Jessica's love story was cut short when they found out that Valerie had a tumor. She was twenty-eight, and that's as long of a life she would be permitted to have. This couple had a short time together, unlike some of the other stories shared in this chapter. It's not that couples who are afforded decades together are ever ready to let go of their life together. They do have more memories together to cling to, more vacations, holidays, birthdays and funny moments, a flurry of inside jokes they shared.

In the reading, Valerie said she reverted to the age of 19, an age where she felt vibrant and full of hope for her future. Valerie talked about Jessica, "wearing her shirts." Jessica then shared she was wearing one for her reading. This was Valerie's way of letting Jessica know that she was not just talking to me, but she was also sitting with her. The first thing that Valerie said was, "I'm sorry, babe." She was sorry that she couldn't hold on any longer. Sorry, they wouldn't walk down the aisle or build a life together. She talked about not being able to think straight when she was dying; her mind was foggy. No doubt because of the pain killers she was taking to make her more comfortable. Valerie showed me herself standing on the beach with a long stick in her hand. She said, "she was writing their names in the sand with the stick and finished it with a heart." Jessica then told me that she had just done this for Valerie. That message was Valerie's way of letting Jessica know that she was with her on the beach writing in the sand too. As a couple, they knew what they had, and they intensely valued their time together. Jessica is having a hard time adjusting to a life with Valerie in spirit. It's a shock to the system when your soul finds what it's been looking for all it's existence, just to have it taken away. It seemed the reading allowed Jessica to connect with her other half in a way that will help redefine their relationship moving forward. I told Jessica that the end of Valerie's life wouldn't have had as much meaning if she hadn't fallen in love with Jessica. She would've died never knowing what it felt like to be passionately loved as Jessica loved her. For those of you who came into someone's life at the end of their life, please remember that you being in their lives, gave them a sweetness that they never would've known without you. Even short love stories can be, forever loves.

All of the readings discussed in this chapter had people from different walks of life, they came from various places, they met at different stages in their lives, but all of the readings had one thing in common. They all happened because the person my clients loved the most, had died. Love binds us together; it's a force that can make our hearts beat, sometimes it can stop our hearts from beating. Love is something that people *want;* we seek it out. If we didn't, there wouldn't be a lot of dating in the world. Once we find it, we fight for it; we cling to it, we don't want to live without it. The same is true when life as we know it ends when half of the magic dies. We will find a way to keep the connection, because without them, the world as we know it, has no light. True love, holds on, we'll wait forever if we have to in order to be together again, time makes it so that we don't have to. For now, the living has to settle for closing our eyes and listening to what they need to say to us or show us in our minds. We must expect signs from them, without dismissing them as something else.

Let them be part of your life; they want to so badly. They hang around and listen to us share stories about them; they love that, the most. They kiss us goodnight, even if you can't see them, your soul knows they're there. Your pets, work overtime to tell you that the person you miss is standing right next to you. They bark, they hiss, they plant themselves right where "Mom" or "Dad" used to sit or sleep. Love keeps the door between the living world and the spirit world, open enough for us to maintain our connection.

A warm thank you to the ladies in this chapter and their soulmates. Thank you for inspiring people who've found love to forever value it, even on the bad days. I hope people who aren't sure love exists, will stay open to the possibility that it might.

MY SOULMATE JOE

I often have trouble finding a unique way to tell Joe that I love him. I've loved him for so long, and so intensely, it seems as though I could do more, find better words. The words "I love you" get thrown around by people who don't mean them, so I strive to find new syllables to tell him how I feel. The best way is probably not to simply say words but rather to show him. I know that he knows that I love him, but for the sake of writing this section for him, I have no choice but to find the words.

When I was looking for an inspirational quote to open this chapter, I found the perfect one. I knew it was the right one because it put into words how I carry Joe in my soul.

"I was always yours to have. You were always mine.

We have loved each other in and out of time."- Maya Angelou

The three sentences that sum up soulmates. The beauty of the poem doesn't mean that soulmates aren't flawed people. We all have our flaws, but we accept each other for our imperfections. Joe knows mine, and I know his. Our flaws are part of what makes up our unique energy; our imperfections can include struggle, other times, our quirks are what drew our mate to us in the first place.

I don't candy-coat my words, and I am clear about my boundaries. When I first met Joe, he knew that about me within 60 seconds. He seemed amused by it. I wasn't expecting him to appreciate a quality in me that usually served me well in getting rid of whoever was hitting on me. The more I got to know him, the clearer it became to me that he was also direct. It quickly became apparent to us that we laughed at things that NOBODY else thought was funny. We found it hysterical. We started looking at each other as if to say, "Where have you been all my life? I thought I was alone in this world."

A soulmate feels similar in energy to "a calling," it's as if when you were created, this person was made to forge a path with you. I always knew that my heart was searching for something; I didn't think it could be a person because I was never going to get married or have kids. I didn't know when I met Joe that he would be my husband. I wasn't in the market for one; I didn't fantasize about getting married. I wasn't one of those little girls who dreamed of it her whole life. Psychic/mediums can't always see or know the future when it comes to ourselves or someone close to us. Honestly, if I had *known* that he was going to be my husband, I might have run. I was only 20 years old, and the last thing that I was looking for was a husband.

There was a time early on in our relationship when Joe held my hand at the movies; I had a strange feeling that told my heart that he was special. We walked down the aisle in the movie theater, and he grabbed my hand to lead me through the people, to our seats. We were only on our 3rd or 4th date. When he wrapped his hand around mine, I instantly felt safe. I felt home. I felt like I *knew* him.

But how could that be? We'd only known each other for a couple of months. There was something electric in that moment that caused me to pause and look at him. I had never felt such a rush of feeling so completely connected to another person before. At that moment, I knew I was precisely where I was supposed to be in life. I felt it; it rushed through his hand into mine. It sort of scared me, because it was a sensation I had never experienced before.

Looking back, being who I am now, I know what happened at that moment. I think falling in love might be when your soul recognizes it's counterpart in another. My soul realized that it belonged with his, us, together. I think that his moment came when he blurted out that he loved me, a little too early in the relation-

ship. It would take several more months for the two of us to figure it out. Something inside of us had known we belonged together, long before our little rebel hearts did.

Joe and I dated for a year before we got married. In that year,
we both tried to walk away from one another. Neither of us fit
into the plan of the other. But, when we were apart, I ached. I'd
be out with my friends sitting in a bar, watching the door. No
matter who walked through the door, I didn't care who was there
if it wasn't him. He felt the same way. There was something magnetic about the two of us. We were great individually but stronger
together.

After we'd been together for almost a year, we were arguing,
and I let the words slip out, "Don't you know, we're supposed to
be together?!"

His answer was, no. He didn't *know* that we were supposed to
be together. When he said it, I was crushed. That must mean he
doesn't love me, I thought. We broke up. Three weeks later, he
was returning from California. He called me on the phone and
asked me to "Wait there, I've made a big mistake."

It was a movie moment. Joe walked in with love in his eyes;
he put his arms around me, spun me around, and kissed me. At
that moment, all of the pieces of my broken heart pulled themselves back together again. He whispered I love you. My soul believed him. We were married in a small ceremony three weeks
later. Twelve months later, we had a big formal wedding. I
looked like a wedding cake in my 90's wedding gown, but we
were happy. Our friends and family were present. We watched
the sunset over the city, from our top floor view at the Plaza
Club, and we danced the night away.

Joe and I have talked about that moment recently. It's been al-most twenty-seven years since it happened. One day he said to me, "I understand now, why you were so hurt when, I told you I didn't *know* for sure that we were supposed to be together."

"Oh, yeah?" I replied.

"You were psychic, and you thought that everyone could see what you could, but they can't. The rest of us have to catch up to find out the things that you see so clearly. So, you thought I did-n't love you, but I did, I knew that. I just didn't plan on getting married until I was thirty-years-old, I couldn't even think five-years ahead, then."

It's funny how couples become more like one another as time goes on. Look at Joe being an introspective, empath! It was an epiphany for both of us, and it explained a lot that has happened in our relationship.

Time is a funny thing; the older we get, the more we can see life from other people's perspectives. The expectations that I'd had for him to read my mind all of those years was unattainable for him. Through my lens, I saw life through the eyes of a psy-chic/medium; that's the only way I had ever seen the world. When I would feel hurt or disappointed that he didn't see or know what I did, it was nothing he could help. It was nothing he could change. Now, we make a real effort to see life through the lens of our partner, which draws us even closer. Joe is my soulmate; he's my leading man; he elevates my soul. Every day that I wake-up and he's there, I feel blessed. I know that time can be unfair. I'm aware that one day, one of us may not be so fortunate to wake up wrapped in the security of the other being there. I've already lived through watching my television character grieve Joe's loss.

It was painful, and that was just actors pretending to be us. We're more than a television show; we're the real love story. I savor every day with my sexy nerd, and I wouldn't trade my life with him for anything in the universe.

The stories shared in this chapter, reflect a once in a lifetime love. The one who can't be replaced or forgotten. The person they ache for, the one who shared inside jokes with them, that nobody else thought was funny. If you have never had a soulmate, you may not understand it's meaning or importance. Some may believe it can't exist. For those who drew the lucky number in this lifetime, you know who you are. You know, your partner's heartbeat, you like to listen to its rhythm. Their smile or laugh, turns up the intensity of the light, in your eyes. You reserved a piece of your soul, long ago, for them. When you met them, fell in love and chose them, you gave them that part of your soul, never to be touched by another. When you have a soulmate, when they are away from you, something inside of you longs to be with them. All of the women who shared their stories here, yearn for their great love, to come back to them. Through their readings with me, I hope that they can now better reach and reconnect with the one who holds their heart—bringing their love back to them in some small measure.

Flirt

S ometimes, widows and widowers get dressed up for their phone reading, so they look nice for their husband or wife. The deceased often mentions in a reading that their living spouse got dressed up for their 'date.' Sometimes, they just say how beautiful their wives look, and other times they say how sexy their wives look still wearing their husband's t-shirt. When conducting phone readings, I've had to convey to my client that her husband says, "she looks great in his shirts."

She'll begin to cry and laugh while telling me that she's wearing his shirt right now! In an instant, the living half of the couple is aware that her love is still with her, sitting beside her, still loving her. A passionate love connection is always felt long after our loved one has physically passed away.

Try being an interpreter between two flirting people who miss each other. Love is the most powerful emotion on earth, it's made me blush on more than a couple of occasions during readings. I've brought through a couple of wives/girlfriends who talked about the 'lingerie they wore.' This evokes a smile from my male client as he gets a knowing grin on his face and shakes his head that he remembers.

One thing about feeling the love between two people in a reading is that sometimes you feel like a voyeur or as if you're crashing their very private party. Some couples just have more of an intensity than others. I never know what kind of reading I'll be dropping in on when my booking assistant hands me my schedule for the week. I'll tell you this, though, giving someone a chance to reconnect with their other half gives me a great sense of purpose. Hearing my client laugh alongside her/his partner with a light heart means everything to me.

MY EYES ADORED YOU

HEATHER AND ANDREW

Heather

I met Andrew through my first husband, Andrew was his karate instructor. From the moment I first saw him, I was sure I loved him. He was the most handsome man at the party. My first husband wasn't very nice to me, and after I finally got the courage to leave him, Andrew became my savior. One night he popped in to see how my daughters, Katharine, Jennifer, Amy, and I were doing. Andrew never left my side from then on. He had challenges with my girls, as they didn't like him entering our lives but slowly realized how wonderful he was. He took on my three girls and my abusive ex-husband. He stood beside me through it all. After a while, we welcomed our baby daughter Samantha, and our family became bonded. My eldest daughter said at our wedding that, if he stayed around after what they put him through then, he must really love us.

It only took a few more years, and my girls realized that although he wasn't their biological father, he was sure *dad* to them. We worked together in his martial arts business, so we were together 24/7, and we loved it. Yes, we argued, but because we loved each other, we didn't stay mad for long. He treated me like a princess, and I loved him as my prince; we were definitely soul mates. He made me a cup of tea every night, and it didn't matter what he was doing, I came first. In fact, everybody loved him. There wasn't anything he wouldn't do to help others, and he always had time to listen to anyone or whoever needed him. I never thought I would ever be without him. When I had my reading with Allison, I was so over the moon, it was if he was in the room with me again.

He thanked me for doing everything I could for him, and he *thanked* me for the words I said to him at the end. I told him that, I would be okay, and it was time for him to let go. Allison said to me that "he was sorry, he couldn't respond" He apologized for "ruining Christmas for me."

He died a month before. It was the time of the year he loved the most, he could never stop giving people presents. Allison also said he told her, "it was his blue eyes that got you, and he misses laughing with me." He had the bluest eyes I had ever seen, and the laughter we shared was the best. We always knew what each other was going to say and shared thoughts. Allison also told me that I was not only his "great love" but also his "best friend," and he told anyone he knew that this was true. He always introduced me as his "lovely, awesome wife!"

In my reading, he said, there was no him, without me, and he "was born to love me" (he always said this to me).

The funniest thing that Allison told me he said, was, "To not sniff the buttons off of his shirts, he sees me doing this!" Me and my daughters, do this to any shirts, we find of his. He always smelled so fragrant, we could smell him coming. She also said that "he sees me going to a great hall on my trip to London, with people dressed up."

I did end up going to the Cirque de Soleil, and it was in a great hall in London the following month.

Allison told me, Andrew said, that "I did everything right, it was a beautiful day, with great food and a lot of people attending his funeral. He liked what I did."

There were over five-thousand people at his funeral! Allison laughed and said, "he was coming through flirting with me and being very romantic."

He was always like this in life, too. Allison told me that he reverted to the age of 32, which was his "heaven on earth."

That's the age he was when we started dating. The anniversary of our first date was June, which he kept making reference to the month of "*June*" in my reading. Allison said he says, "He spends his time around water."

He owned a boat and loved our house by the lake. All of this was true. He said, I wasn't ready to let go of him yet. He made reference to the "shrine" I have of him in my kitchen.

I cannot bear the thought of not having him near me. I never wanted to let him go until I realized that he was wasting away. Allison also made reference to him being "dearly, loved, and respected by a lot of men."

He was a martial arts instructor, he was incredibly loved by all. There was a great sadness stemming from his passing.

I loved the way he came through in my reading, and the words that he said to Allison made me realize that he wasn't gone. I know he is around me, my daughters, and my grandchildren. My reading with Allison gave me great comfort that I am not alone. Andrew is my soul mate, I will never get that again in life, we were meant to be together. Although he came through saying, he doesn't want me to be alone and that at some stage, I am just going to have to *settle* with someone else.

I am currently seeing a wonderful man, but no one *could* ever replace Andrew; he definitely was one of a kind. My girls knew what unconditional love was after Andrew came into our lives. After finally finding love and spending 20 beautiful years with him (I thought many more to be had), I lost the love of my life. I cared for him at home and nursed him with my girls until he passed away in bed. I was holding his hand and hugging him.

Ours was a love story, that sadly ended, too soon. But like Allison told me, "every day that I wake up is a good day, because it's another day closer to being with him again."

My daughter once said, "Mum, I don't ever want to go through life, never experiencing the kind of love you and Dad had."

Some say "soul mates" are a myth, but I know they're real, Andrew was, is, and will always be, my *Soul Mate.*

MY TAKE ON HEATHER'SREADING

I really vibed with Heather. Throughout her reading, her husband, Andrew, flirted with her and tried to make her laugh. One of the perks of being a medium is that you get to feel the intensity of the love between your client and the spirit whispering in your ear. When Heather would laugh at something Andrew said, I could feel her mood lighten. Her laugh reassured Andrew, that their connection was intact and that he could still pluck the strings in her heart. Andrew felt to me, as though his positivity and strength could lift up anyone with a withering belief in themselves. I'm sure he had done this many times for all he touched. When he initially came through in the reading, he said, he's loving, warm, and funny.

I could tell by Heather's reaction to him, that all of these descriptions were true. He also felt like a leader to me, unafraid of most. When I bring through, people with "leader" energy, they make me feel a sense of fearlessness. In readings, making contact with "leader" energy actually makes me take a deep breath and hold it in for a few seconds—with the feeling of filling up with pride and certainty. Followers, don't feel that way when they come through. They have an energy that smacks of uncertainty, with a hint of self-deprecation. This is a little Mediumship 101 lesson for those of you who are trying to understand how to read energies that come through you.

Not only did Andrew say that he "reverted to the age of 32" but also that, he liked how he "looked in his swim trunks."

Heather commented that he looked great in his swimsuit.

I'm sure there are some pictures of him at 32, that he'd like Heather to take out and remember him by. Rather than her thinking of how he looked when he was sick and deteriorating. In every reading, that I conduct, the dead talk about the age they revert to, their "version of heaven on earth."

Andrew's version of heaven was the age he was when he met and fell in love with Heather.

He spoke of his father being with him.

This was important because his father had died three weeks after, Andrew. Recent passings are often acknowledged in readings, so the family knows they're okay. Also, that they're with the person I initially brought through. Although he talked about many aspects of his life in the reading, he seemed mostly worried about his family. Mostly his wife and all of his beautiful daughters. He spoke of his daughter Amy, naming her daughter, after him, and how honored he was to share his name. He had messages for them all, but I think what Andrew really wanted them all to know was the same sentiment that Heather had said to him when he died.

"I love you, and it will be okay."

This love story shared two people coming together and crafting a life together, merging two lives into one. Heather's reading stood out to me because there was an active flirtation between her and her husband throughout the reading. I find the synergy between flirting people to be sweet and youthful, no matter how old they are, the love is young.

Heather shared her feelings and innermost thoughts with us to reach a reader who may be missing their love. The hope of everyone who shared a story in my book was that their story would resonate with others—people who are grieving and maybe not as far down the road of healing, quite yet. Maybe hearing accounts of other people's losses, and reconnecting with them in spirit will open you up to connecting with someone you love.

Heather's story captured the unwavering strength of their love. Love is electric, it's renewable energy with no end. Some relationships have more heat, more sizzle than others, love can make us feel emotions that we didn't even know that we had inside of us! What love does to all of us is that it leaves us feeling a deep sense of having to be with that one person; because there's no one like them in all the world. We have no choice; the alternative is to go back to a life that will never feel whole without that person.

FIGHTING FOR LOVE

BELLA AND MICHAEL

Bella

I was at the gym doing overhead kicks and mimicking body-blow punches when I felt an overwhelming stare coming from someone exercising behind me. You know the feeling you get when you're stopped at a red light, and feel the intense glare of the person in the car next to you that compels you to turn your head and look at them? It felt just like that, but even more urgent.

I tried to ignore the strong pull to turn around to look at whoever was staring at me. I was really working out hard, sweat dripping down from my forehead into my eyes, so I ignored the source. After several minutes of fighting the impulse to turn around and find out who was looking at me, I finally gave in to the annoying distraction and stopped my workout. I turned around and moved my head from side to side to visually locate the person staring me down. My eyes locked with a man's eyes who were glaring at me. A powerful electric shot went through my stomach like a lightning bolt, causing me to actually double over at the waist and gasp to take my next breath.

I had never felt such an overpowering physical sensation in my stomach like that before. I was no stranger to being kicked and punched in the stomach, being a personal trainer and a self-defense teacher for women. The feeling was so strong that I had to go down on one knee for a moment. I kneeled, looking down at the ground, trying to figure out what had just happened to my body. I heard a voice begin to introduce himself as Michael and explain that he was looking for a trainer to help him improve his golf game (to qualify for the PGA Tour), I stood up. We shook hands, exchanged numbers, and agreed to meet at a convenient location later on that evening to hammer out the necessary details concerning training goals.

That evening we both arrived fifteen minutes early. Michael

quoted Vince Lombardi as I walked up to him and stuck out my hand to shake his. He said, "If you are five minutes early, you are already ten minutes late."

"Do you know who said that Bella?" he questioned.

I replied, "Vince Lombardi."

My correct response elicited a smile from Michael. There was something so sexy about his grin, something so electric!

I scored major points for being there ahead of schedule, so my hiring interview was off to a great start! Michael required a trainer who could start at 4:45 a.m., Monday through Friday. The time was non-negotiable since he needed to be on the tee, by 7 a.m. The local gyms I explained did not open their doors to the public until 5 a.m. Michael said, "then we will meet outside the gym at 4:45 a.m. and work on core exercises like planks, mountain climbers, push-ups, and crunches until the gym opened."

I got up around 3am every morning to go running, so getting to the club to train him at such an early hour was no big deal.

Michael and I shook hands, to close the deal. As we grasped hands to shake, Michael squeezed my fingers firmly and said, "I am never late, never."

Feeling slightly irritated at what I conferred was his insinuation that I was the type to be late to an appointment. I retorted, "Well, I never date my clients either, not ever!"

Michael smiled that heart-stopping smile and chuckled, as we released each other's hands and parted company.

For the next month, Michael and I met at the gym at 4:45 a.m. Monday through Friday. He was, in fact, never late. I, on the other hand, was late a couple of times. On those few occasions, Michael would look at his phone's time and smile from ear-to-ear with a Cheshire grin and mutter, "Lombardi time, Bella."

He made my Italian temper flare up immediately because he was right. At the same time, he coaxed a belly laugh out of me that nearly gave me a stitch in my side. Michael was a hilarious guy, he always tried to make people laugh.

After four weeks of hard training, Michael up and fired me following our Friday morning workout. I worked so hard with him, improving his long drive and short game, both putting and chipping. He had said so himself on several occasions. I was flabbergasted as to why he was letting me go. "What did I do wrong?" I whispered in my head. Michael thanked me sincerely for working with him and paid me what he owed me. I was terribly upset to be losing such a great client. Still, I hid my feelings outwardly, not making any facial gestures. I handled being fired, like a true professional.

As I turned to walk to my truck, Michael called out to me, hollering over several parked cars. "Since I'm not your client anymore, I would like very much to take you out to dinner, Bella. I want to know everything, there is to know about you."

I began hysterically laughing because of Michael's cleverness and how he totally blindsided me with his dinner proposal. I never saw it coming. How methodical he was to fire me, only to ask me out on a date. I basically couldn't say no, because he was no longer a client of mine, and did I mention, sexy?

That first date began what turned out to be the most meaningful seven and a half year romance, of my entire life! One that swept me off my feet, he captured my heart, as well as my soul. Michael and I were sweethearts in the most real sense of the word. He became the love of my life, and he told me more times than I could ever count: "You are the love of my life. I loved you more than I love myself, more than *life* itself even."

Michael and I were inseparable. We went to bed entwined with both our arms and legs snaking around one another, holding each other in a snuggling embrace. We slept like two peas in one pod. I don't know how we ever slept like that, but we did, for over seven years. We did everything together. We ran on the beach together. Trained at the gym alongside each other. If one of us went somewhere, the other one came too.

A month before Michael died, we got engaged. We had talked about getting married a dozen times during our seven and a half year relationship. Michael said he felt *married* to me. I definitely felt *married* to him in my heart. We wanted to get married, but we were both pretty skittish over actually going to the courthouse and saying, "I do."

Michael and I had each been married before; both marriages ended in painful divorces. Needless to say, we were both more than a little gun shy. There was also something else that prevented Michael and me from getting married. Michael was an alcoholic. He would stay sober for six months or more, but then he would go out with a friend after golf and have a cocktail or think he could drink a couple of cold beers during a football or basketball game. One or two drinks would start a terrible bout of drinking. This resulted in my taking care of him for several days, helping him withdraw from alcohol, and attempting another chance at sobriety.

I wanted to marry Michael with all of my heart, but I didn't want to be married to a drunk. I knew that would be hell on earth. I had two uncles who died due to their alcoholism. I didn't want the horrible kind of life that I saw growing up. When Michael asked me to marry him, I said, "Yes" and cried tears of joy.

He said, "When?"

I said, "When you can go without drinking for seven straight days, we'll get married."

Michael agreed.

I have since regretted not marrying Michael, immediately after he asked me. The month, before he died. I was so angry at myself for putting off our marriage until he was sober. He wanted to make me his wife and I wanted with every piece of my heart, for him to be my husband. Now, it was too late.

The last month that Michael was alive, he struggled to get sober, over and over again. He was sober for several days staying clean, and then he'd slip up. He said the withdrawal, the headaches, nausea, dizziness, and tiredness were too much at times. He would go out to buy alcohol when I was working. I would come home to find him drunk or passed out. I would sadly clean him up, put him in bed, bring him water, and feed him soup or soft food until he felt better. This ugly cycle repeated from October to early November. Michael was drinking when he accidentally fell and hit his head. He hit it hard enough, in just the right spot, to cause a fatal subdural hematoma. It killed him while I was at work. I came home to find my mate, the love of my life, and the man who was to be my husband, the father of my future children, dead.

The bottom had dropped out from under me. Michael was the one who wrapped himself around me like a blanket every night. He was my workout partner. Michael was the bounce in my step as we ran on the beach. He was the smiling face across the dinner table from me. With his death, I felt so very alone.

As time passed following Michael's death, his funeral, and finally his cremation, the realization that Michael was gone from my life began to creep in. I missed my mate's presence in my daily life. I could hardly get out of bed each morning. Trying to cope with his absence, I hung up a couple of his pictures in my bathroom. I wanted to see his handsome reflection looking at me in the mirror while I was putting on my perfume and make-up like I used to be able to do as he shaved in the mirror next to me. The pictures made me feel better. Especially, the one with Michael standing underneath a bunch of palm trees, with his shirt off. The picture looked like it was taken in Hawaii, one of the places we had planned to travel to soon. Now, all I had was an engagement ring to remind me of our plans for the beautiful, exciting life, we had hoped to spend together.

I wasn't processing my grief very well. I had never been much of a crier, but my devastated heart caused me to sob uncontrollably at night, as I lay in a half-empty bed that was cold and void. In the car during the day, I periodically screamed out Michael's name, out of sheer loneliness and frustration. I was forced to sing solo to one of our favorite songs that came on the radio. I felt utterly lost without him, and I didn't know how to make the pain I felt, stop.

It was when I was at my lowest, that strange things started happening that had never occurred before. My phone called itself, while it was sitting on the seat next to me in my truck with nothing whatsoever touching it. When I picked it up, no one was there. The phone also started frequently lighting up for no reason at all. The screensaver with Michael's picture would cause me to look at his smiling face and think of happier times. At first, I thought my phone was broken, and that's why it was acting weird. Then I started finding change everywhere I went. It was the nuttiest thing. When I would pull into a parking space at the grocery store, as I would open my car door, I would find pennies, dimes, and nickels outside my car door, peppering the ground. I would have to step on them to exit my car because there were so many of them. If I went out to dump the garbage, I would randomly find pennies, dimes, and nickels, scattered around the garbage cans.

The unpredictable phone and the random barrage of coins weren't enough to make me a believer in the *afterlife*. I didn't believe Michael was trying to send me messages from the great beyond. When I started smelling his cologne and getting sudden hair-raising, cold chills, all over my body in the kitchen, in my bathroom, or while laying in bed, I started to ask aloud, "Michael, is that you?"

Following my spoken questions, I often heard a reply of "Hi, Bella" or "Bella, I love you" would pop into my head and reverberate in my heart.

I was hoping it was really Michael speaking to me and not my mind imagining things, but I wasn't 100% positive. I must sadly admit, I still had my doubts. I finally believed I wasn't making things up in my head when I started having lucid dreams about Michael. They felt absolutely real, not like a dream. On several occasions, I woke up frantically, calling out his name loudly, looking around for him in my bedroom. I could have sworn I felt him physically holding me like he used to when we slept.

All of these paranormal experiences collectively caused me to seek out answers about what happened after death. I went to the book store in hopes of finding a book on the subject. I had never heard of Allison DuBois before, nor had I heard the word "medium" before, except regarding clothing size. Allison's book titled *We Are Their Heaven* caught my eye, I bought it. As I read it, I started to recognize similarities to what I was experiencing, described within its pages. I went back and purchased another book written by Mrs. DuBois called *Secrets of the Monarch*. This book also provided numerous examples of serendipitous instances, that bordered on the supernatural and the divine. The stories spoke to my heartache and lessened my grief by furnishing me with even more descriptions that resembled my own life. I went on to purchase *Talk to Me*, followed by *Into the Dark*, and finally, *Don't Kiss Them Good-Bye*. Each book helped me to cry a little bit less, each night, to not feel so alone and depressed during the day. I started to honestly believe and not merely *think* that I felt Michael's spiritual presence.

I had finally finished reading Allison's books and scrutinizing many other books written by medical doctors and those with PhDs on end-of-life and afterlife phenomena. I finally got the courage to dismiss what my friends and family had said about there being no life after death. I instead, went with what my heart was telling me to do. I emailed Allison DuBois's assistant and asked for a 30-minute Mediumship reading for Allison to bring through Michael, my love, my fiancé.

I had to wait several weeks before Allison had the scheduling opportunity to conduct my reading. When the day came, Allison called me right on time, which I very much appreciated. I sat next to the phone in great anticipation, flipping through pictures of

Michael and reading a few of the cards that he had given me through the years. Allison asked me the relationship of the person that I wanted her to bring through. I said, "My mate." Allison went quiet, and in a few minutes, Allison said, she had him.

The reading began with Allison asking me, "Had you already gone shopping for rings?" We had, in fact, gone shopping for wedding rings. We had looked at several. We agreed on three which Michael took pictures of and stored on his phone.

I said to Allison, "We had." I choked, trying to say the words, "We just didn't have time to get it."

Allison began speaking the words she heard Michael saying to her. "He wants you to have the ring. He thinks you need it, like to wear it. You need to have that connection to him. So have you thought of going to get the ring?"

I whimpered out a sorrowful, "Yes."

I had contemplated in my head several times about going to the jewelry store and buying the wedding ring that went with my engagement ring. The compulsion was there, but I had shoed it away each time. Allison continued, "It's what he's urging you to do. He thinks it's important for the two of you to come *full circle* if you will."

Allison was kind enough to break up my tears with a joke that a wedding ring is a circle, and it would bring us full circle. I wiped my tears and laughed with her. I sat still, mesmerized that Michael talked about my getting my wedding ring. It was as if he had been reading my thoughts—the ones I had been having for several weeks.

Allison next said Michael was showing her the number 32. "Did he make it past the age of 32?" Allison asked me.

I said that he had. Allison then told me that Michael had put his hand on top of his head to signify that his hair was now perfect. I chuckled into the phone. Michael had been very sensitive to the fact that he started losing his hair at a relatively early age. Michael always liked the pictures of him in his early 30's, because he still had a head full of really great-looking brown hair, at that age. Those were the exact pictures that I had repeatedly been thumbing through, since Michael's passing. All the images of him were from when he was around the age of 32. When Allison told me that she felt like Michael was trying to let me know that he had been there with me, as I was looking through the pictures of him longingly.

Michael says it's his smile that really got to you.

I was shocked that Allison said precisely what I had told Michael when he won my heart during the burgeoning of our relationship. Allison shared with me that Michael told her that the two of us just made a lot of sense together. Michael always told his friends and family when describing our relationship: "Bella and I make a lot of sense together. We understand one another."

Allison repeated these two exact phrases that helped me to understand that Michael still had clear memories of what I had said to him. Those words were so significant to us both. Allison was honestly speaking to my Michael.

"There were a lot of things that he still wanted to do with you. He's showing himself standing on the beach under a palm tree. It feels like Hawaii was supposed to come into play for the two of you."

I told Allison that I have a picture in my bathroom of Michael standing underneath several palm trees and wearing swimming trunks on hard white pressed sand. I kissed it many a morning and thought about that trip to Hawaii that we were hoping to take someday. Allison told me, it was a trip that Michael still wanted me to take.

She recommended that I take a trip to Hawaii with a girlfriend and prop up a picture of Michael, when I got there and say, "We made it."

"It's important to him," Allison uttered.

Allison then told me, she asked Michael what he felt, around the time that he died. Allison said, "He seemed confused as to what was going on at the time he passed, and he pointed to his head and made my head hurt. Was there head pain for him at the time that he passed?"

"That's what killed him," I painfully stated.

"Okay, but then it feels like it was over, but he gave me a feeling of confusion in the moments leading up to his death. I don't know if it was his own thoughts that were cloudy or if something was happening around him confusing him. It feels like he didn't have a grasp of what was happening, what was going on."

Even though I believed wholeheartedly, Allison brought Michael through. She spoke his words, sharing pictures with me, that he was showing her. I was still floored that Allison was able to describe Michael's head injury and the cause of his death. There was no other way that she could have known. Allison didn't know Michael's first or last name. Allison only was told that she was bringing through "my mate, my fiancé."

As the reading progressed, I received confirmation after confirmation that Michael was speaking through Allison. Michael remembered so many of the most essential details of our relationship. Allison told me things that only Michael and I knew. She repeated statements that Michael and I had said to one another during intimate moments of embrace. She said, "He said it took forever for him to find you. And sometimes he didn't even know what you saw in him, but he was grateful to have you."

Warm tears streamed down my face as I recalled the actual moments that I was in my soulmate's arms, as he poured out his heart and professed his love to me.

Sadness turned into laughter, as Allison chuckled and said, "He says, he's in your phone. He's laughing. Like he's posing for a picture. You have his picture on your phone, or he's your screensaver. He's saying that his energy is in your phone. Also, you miss calling him, he says."

I replied, "Very much."

"You may look at his phone number still. He's going through it with you, but trying to assure you that he's going to hold your hand every day of your life, until you don't need him to hold it anymore. He says you're not meant to be alone. You're meant to be loved. He's clear on that."

"This isn't anything that you may be ready for, Bella," she said, "He doesn't feel like you should spend the rest of your life by yourself. He says he loves you too much."

I was able to verify the accuracy of what Allison was saying by the phrase, "You're meant to be loved."

Michael had looked me in the eyes on our anniversary and said those exact words to me. This was Michael, making sure that I knew he meant what he was saying through Allison.

"He says you took such good care of him. He felt so loved."

I replied, "Good, I tried."

Allison said, "He knew." Allison then told me, "He says he misses the simple things, like going out to dinner with you. He misses going out to dinner and talking about your day and making plans. You were his heaven. You were his version of heaven."

Michael had said nearly those exact words several weeks before he died. I had been working my two jobs, virtually six days a week, from early morning until dark. He had said numerous times to me, "I miss going out to dinner with you, Bella, and hearing you talk about your day. I miss making plans together." When Allison told me what Michael had shared with her, I knew Michael's personality, memories, and desires were still perfectly intact, wherever he was in spirit.

"He keeps trying to get you to go back to the beach. He says, go to the water." Tears welled up in my eyes, and I sniffed into the phone after hearing that Michael told Allison that he kept trying to get me to go back to the beach. I began to cry because now I understood why two people that I hardly knew at the gym came up to me within days of one another and asked me, if I wanted to go to the beach?

Michael was somehow able to whisper into the ears of two individuals and ask me to go to the beach. He did this to get me back to where we spent so many magical moments, walking hand-in-hand, and we made out like lovesick teenagers. Allison told me that when I wonder what Michael is doing, sometimes "he's running on the beach with you, reliving the moments he spent with you."

Allison continued the reading by telling me, "Sometimes

when you wake up and think he was just there, it's because he was. When you sleep, he puts his arms around you, and he holds you. So he hasn't left you. He stayed."

I thanked Allison and said, "I can't tell you how many times that has happened, and I said his name out loud."

Allison answered me and said, "Yes, he was there. It's like you were just having a moment with him, and then you woke up. It might even be a frantic moment where you want to go back to sleep because you want to experience it again, you know? But he says that he will continue to hold you."

"He feels funny to me, he liked to make you laugh or that he enjoyed making people laugh in general. He feels like a great guy. He is comparing himself to — I don't know if you've ever seen the movie *Top Gun*, there's a scene where the character Goose and Tom Cruise are singing, 'You've lost that loving feeling,' and he feels like that kind of guy to me. It feels like he was a mix of Tom Cruise's character Maverick and the character Goose if you blended their two personalities together."

After Allison finished describing what Michael was showing and telling her, I let out a huge burst of laughter. Michael and I had watched this movie in bed many times over the years. His favorite part of the movie, as well as mine, was the bar scene, where Maverick and Goose serenade Kelly McGillis. Michael always said he was as cute as Tom Cruise and as hilarious as Goose. Of course, I agreed that Michael was equally as good looking as Tom Cruise and just as funny as Goose. Once again, I knew that Michael was sharing an endearing memory to tell me that his self-confidence and humor were still intact.

After several seconds of Allison and I laughing together, Allison got quiet for a few moments. She then said very seriously, "He says that you're the love of his life. He doesn't need to say that out loud, for you to know that it's true. He says he just likes to hear it."

I giggled to Allison because of the truth of what she was conveying to me. I had told family and friends, dozens, if not a hundred times in the months since Michael's passing, that it was hard to lose the love of my life.

I had quietly questioned if I had indeed been the love of his life since I was mad at him for dying on me, the way he did. Michael was letting me know that he was still around me and able to hear what I was saying about him; he knows my private thoughts and feelings. What Allison told me, brought me so much comfort. I knew that I was the love of Michael's life, it was meaningful to hear it from him, one more time, from Allison's lips.

Allison then said, "He says, *children*. Had you wanted to have children?"

"Yes," I cried.

"He says that you were born to be a mother, you were supposed to be a mom. He wanted that for you, and you wanted that *with* him. He wishes that he could give that to you. Everything got cut short. It was just so abrupt. It feels like it was out of nowhere when it happened, so there's trauma there. There's trauma for you and for him, also."

Moments before my reading with Allison, I read several cards that Michael had given me that year. The Mother's Day before he died, Michael had given me a Mother's Day card. He wrote in it that he wished that he had children with me. The card was one of my favorites because it spoke of the children that we had wanted to have together. Allison telling me that, let me know that Michael was with me, minutes before Allison had telephoned me. He was letting me know that he saw me reading the card and remembering how we wanted a family.

Allison also told me, "He says that you would do well, with a curly white-haired dog."

It's a feeling as though you need a friend.

I shook my head and laughed out of shock that Michael had told Allison that. On several consecutive days leading up to my reading, I had gone to the county animal shelter. I looked at adopting a cat or a dog. I left, empty-handed each time, because I could not make up my mind, whether I should bring home a feline or a canine. I also couldn't make up my mind about whether I wanted an entirely white or an entirely black-haired pet. I was in utter amazement that once again, Michael had shared with Allison, something fairly recent. Something that I was thinking about and contemplating. Michael helped me understand that he was able to read my thoughts and my feelings and pass on information to me of what he knew, I needed to hear.

The entire thirty minutes that Allison conducted my reading, she said one thing after another, that Michael had said to me while he was alive or told me something that he had seen me do or think since he passed. Allison told me about the birthday cake that Michael was showing her, he said to her that he liked what I gave him. I had gone ahead and celebrated Michael's birthday with a colorful birthday cake and candles after he died, even though Michael never liked celebrating his birthday.

Allison was also able to tell me that Michael said he was in the afterlife, with my father and my Uncle Bill.

Allison told me that fact should bring me comfort. Because now, I could picture all of the men who loved me. They were together able to share their common bond, their love for me. Michael confirmed the accuracy of what Allison shared with me by explaining that it was my father, who was the one leaving me all the coins. Allison asked me, who the William or Bill connection associated with my father was? She asked if I had an Uncle Bill?

My father and brother, my Uncle Bill, had passed on before Michael's death. Michael told Allison to tell me that "the three of them were playing golf together on a beautiful golf course."

I was shocked. I squealed with laughter and astonishment when Allison said the three of them were playing golf together in the afterlife.

Michael had been a scratch player hoping to one day qualify for the PGA Tour. To think that he was playing golf with my dad and uncle (who were not great golfers) in the afterlife was hysterical to me.

My reading with Allison has changed my life. Knowing that Michael is with me every day in spirit, has stopped most of my crying. I now seem to cry, only happy tears. The knowledge that the love of my life can see me, hear my words, read my thoughts, and put his spiritual arms around me at night, has made me start living again. Thanks to Allison, I live each day with a grateful heart, knowing that there is life after death. I breathe happily with the thought every day that I move one step closer to seeing Michael again. The love of my life, the man who holds my heart, is not my past. He is my future.

MY TAKE ON BELLA'S READING

Michael came through fast and easy, this is not uncommon, with people who have prominent personalities. I love readings, like Bella and Michael's, because I don't have to use all of my energy to connect with them. When the deceased has a strong personality, and the love shared was deep, it takes less energy to communicate with them. The reason is that stronger personalities project louder energy so, all I have to do is listen to them talk and take notes. People who have subdued or more monotone energy require more of my energy to decipher their messages. I have to probe their feelings (because they're not clearly projecting them), and the pictures they show me appear more faded, more challenging to read. It doesn't matter how old they were when they died, or how low on energy they were at the end of their life.

The power that comes through in a reading is the nexus of who they were, at the most vibrant times in their lives. Such as their creative, free-spirited energy in childhood. When they played with endless energy, appreciating something as small as a caterpillar on a leaf or admiring clouds shaped like animals. The deceased can have adrenaline pinching military energy. Constructed from the camaraderie they felt with other soldiers, their heartfelt loyalty, and finding courage within them, they didn't know they had. Sometimes our nexus is a combination of life experiences. It is constructed from the emotions of falling in love, being in love, having children, significant accomplishments, friendships, and relationships with their family. The most moving parts of their lives come together to form the core of who they are; those moments turn into their life force. Most people come through quickly because fun personalities and loving people are often missed more by the living. So they're most of the energies, I experience. People with lower frequency energies aren't requested quite as often for readings. But, when they are, I do my best to pass on their messages. Michael was a passionate person, a sensitive person, who sometimes struggled to cope with this complicated world. His love for Bella was real, he had a big heart full of love, and that's all it took to fuel the reading. He came through chatty and happy to be heard. It was an honor to bring Michael and Bella together again. But, like I always say, "I'm just a secretary!" I take notes from the deceased, and I pass the messages on to the living.

As a footnote, I initially had Michael and Bella's reading in chapter one because theirs truly is a love story of soulmates. I later felt it belonged in chapter two, Flirt. While editing her section, I could *feel* how attracted they were to one another when I'd skim over what she wrote. Starting at the beginning of her story when Michael was watching Bella work out at the gym (clearly admiring her) all the way to the end of the reading. Bella spoke of how physically and emotionally intertwined she and Michael were, even while sleeping. I just sensed a powerful magnetic pull between the two of them coming through in their reading. They had a very intense connection. Every couple has a different *heat* between them. Michael and Bella's showed as they spoke of how they will always love one another. I have no doubt that he will wait for her, and she will be seeing him again.

Write a note to someone you love.

_____

_____

_____

_____

_____

_____

Do We Always Choose Our Partner After Death?

*P*eople who stay together out of obligation, not love, will go their separate ways when they pass. Even if they were married for 50 years. They usually go back to a time before they met their spouse, a time when they had no obligations. If they longed for another unrequited love, they eventually could find them on the Otherside. People who married for money or status and not love can also say au revoir! When I have a client who has been married for 50 years to a man, they say they "never really loved," and "they knew it when they were walking down the aisle." To paraphrase the clients who utter sentences such as these, they say they can't stand him, but they took a vow. Although I respect them for keeping their word, I am acutely aware that they forfeited their life. It's their choice but imagine all of the loveless nights spent lying next to someone they didn't even like. Sharing life's precious moments with someone and not gazing at them with a knowing look of being in love with one another, would feel hollow—no writing of sweet words. No Christmas kiss under the mistletoe, listening to the song "Santa Baby" together? It happens.

On the flipside of marrying someone you don't love are people who have found true love, to quote MEDIUM, "there's no me, without you."

Those who cease to exist once their true love dies. The ones who *will* themselves to die, so they can be reunited in death. The real ending to the fairytale is that you get to be with your other half forever when you crossover. Most likely, they'll be the first person you see when the veil thins. You will relive falling in love, getting married, naming your children, decorating the Christmas tree, whatever your version of heaven on earth was. If you met later in life, I've noticed that often the first one in the couple to die will revert back to an age that predated when they met their partner. They go back to the age they wish they'd met their soulmate. They say things such as, "When you die, we can be young together, as if we had met earlier. You can be a young bride, I'll be a young man eager to start his life with you. We can start over."

They seem to be able to go back and live the life they longed to have together. We're always lucky to meet our soulmates at any age, but those who meet later in life often wish they were able to be young together. To have children together. To experience young love together.

I selfishly love the readings involving people in love, in the early 1960s. They show me how they dressed up for everything, even grocery shopping. Red lipstick, looking so glamorous on a young woman's lips, almost seeming like a warning to men. A warning that will be ignored by every man who gazes upon her face when she smiles. I can hear the music playing, as they dance in a smoky lounge with a band's soft music covering the stage and spilling out on to the dance floor. The cocktails look so dangerous (in a good way), and the music's pulse, coupled with falling in love, is intoxicating. I've experienced people falling in love during WWII. A beautiful young nurse bandaging a soldier's wounds and keeping him company, as he heals. The years start to blend, and I find myself hearing a song by a young Elvis Presley, as I witness a kiss at a Sock Hop, that leads to marriage. I've gazed through my client's eyes as the years peel away, while a widow remembers meeting a young man wearing a leisure suit. When they met, his presence evoked an eye roll from her and her girlfriends, in a disco tech, all those years ago. Love brings us right back to every moment in our life that we thanked God for the partner who made our life's story, overflowing with meaning. It's easy to get lost in our happy memories. They are the exciting, flawed, happy, defining moments, that color the fabric of our lives. The memories that took an ordinary life made it sparkle and turned it into an extraordinary life!

People also ask me, "What if someone was married more than once?"

If someone was married more than once, they go back to the person that they feel they have unfinished business with. This can mean that they still are in love with that person, who may have died young. When a great love dies young, imagine what life would have been like if they hadn't. How different life would have been if they lived. Maybe the living partner never got to say good-bye, and they feel as though they need to see the one who died and tell them how much they meant to them. People marry for various reasons, some were only head over heels in love with one spouse, but another was a great stepdad or breadwinner. Same with why men marry, some want a motherly influence for their children. Some men just want someone to take care of them, share meals with and enjoy good conversation.

When we die, if we were married multiple times, we gravitate to the person who brought us the most joy or who we still feel we need to talk to about how life ended. When we die, we're simply emotionally based beings. We drop egos and chips on our shoulder, we stop blaming others, for how our life unfolded. We're reduced to the best part of us. Your senses become heightened, your ability to love is effortless. Every interesting object you appreciated in life waits for you on the Otherside. The many sounds you heard and marveled over, the gorgeous scents that you took in that caused you to inhale more deeply the second time, wait for you. All that you touched, and admired; become part of your world, once again.

Our soulmates, definitely wait for us. When I bring the romantic mates through for my clients, I love it when they describe the date they're waiting to take their partner on, when they see them again. Sometimes they plan dinner and a movie, sometimes it's a red linen-draped cocktail table close to the stage, waiting for a couple of lovebirds for a night of cold drinks and good music! It's whatever they did together, whatever they miss. They make plans for the day when we join them beyond the veil.

I Love You More!

*C*hildren who die want to remain part of the family. They want their parents to hold them in their hearts and embrace them. While continuing to include them in their daily lives. They still desire to vacation with their family and live vicariously through them! They desperately want to have an ice cream cone with their mom, like they use to and grill burgers with Dad in the summer, at sunset. They're not ready to let go of us, just as we're not ready to let go of them. The trick to re-connection is to meet them in the middle.

Sometimes a *soulmate* comes in the form of a child. Parents love their children more than anything, but there are times when it feels like you knew each other in another lifetime. Some souls keep finding their way back to one another, over and over again. When you die, you relive the happiest days of your life with the people you love who preceded you in death. On the Otherside, we run through the memories that defined our lives as though they're being lived for the first time, savoring the magical memories that got us through dark days. After you die, you will protect your living loved ones through intervention and guidance, waiting to help them over when they pass away. Once there are no living loved ones left to protect, some souls have seemed to recycle back into the world, living in a different time than they knew before. Some souls yearn for a connection with another and search for something or someone out there in that big world, they're not sure what, who, or where they'll find what their heart is searching for, they're not even sure if it really exists? There are times when we have to fall in love to create that cosmic magic that makes us feel complete. A force of nature, the missing piece of the jigsaw puzzle in our heart, sometimes takes our child's form.

Some parents have this soul connection with their child, this closeness, the answer to what had always been missing. The child who becomes their best friend, their mini-me, some would say, their soulmate. I think that most children are our 'soulmate' on some level. Losing such a precious and unique relationship is unfathomable to most of us. Still, some people don't get to be simply spectators to this enormous pain. They are participants, living with an all-consuming loss. They live with the pain every minute, of every hour, of every day. Losing a child makes many parents want to throw in the towel and leave an agonizing existence. They don't fear death, they welcome it. They know that they found a soulmate in this lifetime, and now the world no longer holds joy, has no color or meaning, without that person in it. In the whole world, there was only that one person, who made them feel alive, and going back to life without them, feels like going back to an empty room. I've read thousands of parents over the last twenty years; they all want to have their kids back or to trade places with them. Occasionally, a parent will use the word *soulmate* to describe their child. There was a 'knowing' by the parent from the time that beautiful soul entered the world. They knew their life had become whole at that moment. The tiny eyes that looked up at them for the first time confirmed completeness in the family. There would be no more searching for a phantom love or purpose out in the world, all you ever needed, was staring back at you. To lose, a presence in your life that is rare and beautiful is enough to derail any parent's life.

For me, looking into the eyes of a parent whose child died (sometimes multiple children), sends a dagger right through my heart. They look like they're holding their breath, it's as though the parent doesn't even breathe anymore, as if they're not in the world of the living. The anguish inside of them is like no other earthly pain. It's as though they're screaming inside, and no one can hear them. So they suffer inside, every day, waiting to die, so they can be with their baby again. My job is to listen to their screams and show them another way to reach their child. So, they can re-join the living and complete a full life, seeing their deceased child, the way I see them. Parents who lose children, get stuck in the moments at the end of their child's life. They see them lifeless for the first time, over and over again, they constantly replay their child's funeral in their mind. Some even become determined to feel their child's last moments of life. They want to personally experience any fear or pain their child felt and take it all away. Parents hold on to their child's death because it was the last tangible thing to connect them to their child. They're traumatized, they no longer live in the same world that we do.

They feel like they're outside a glass bubble looking in, watching people who have never known their pain, go on with life without a care in the world. They yearn to feel void of pain again, complaining about the little things that don't really matter and sleeping soundly. But, they realize that life as they knew it will never be that way again, not in this lifetime.

When I conduct a reading, the dead always tell me the age they reverted to what they look like now. So, the living loved one can take out a picture of them at that age to see them now. We revert to the age that was our 'heaven on earth,' a time that was our zenith. When the deceased fell in love, got married, had children, sometimes when they won a prizefight or did something historical, a time of euphoria on earth usually centers around. Even if they got a divorce, they often go back to that relationship in death if they were truly in love or regret not staying with that person. People who pass from suicide, usually go back to childhood, before their chemical imbalance took hold of them; or before they started self-medicating. The visual image for the living and remembrance that their loved one was incredibly happy in their life helps to chip away at their wall of pain. As that wall comes down, the living is more accessible to the dead. It's easier for the dead to be seen and heard by the living if they don't have to contend with an emotional wall. Parents are usually the last ones to receive communication directly. The reason is that the parents are the most severely, emotionally, traumatized. Often, the deceased have to pass messages through other people, to their mom and dad. Trauma has a way of blocking healing from happening because your soul is in shock, it's paralyzed. Paralysis of your very life force (your soul) makes you impenetrable to the dead, rendering them unable to reach you. The wall of pain around you is too thick, and your soul has 'shut down' because it can't take one more painful experience, you've gone into, 'self-protection mode.' Also, because there's a part of the parent who can't come to terms with the loss. Part of the parent's heart is still waiting for their child to walk through the front door. A piece of the parent's soul exists waiting for the phone to ring with a chipper, "Hi, Mom!" on the other end. The walls of pain partnered with the need for their child to still be alive is too much blockage for the Otherside to penetrate. For the parent to accept that their child isn't coming back, is to admit that they're dead. Often, parents are just not ready to accept that yet. It takes a long time to get there.

My Son

Melissa and Dimitri

Melissa

My name is Melissa Lee. I had my first reading with Allison on December 2, 2015. It was approximately 5 months after the passing of my son, Dimitri, on June 30, 2015. As a mother, I have found the most enduring gift one could receive, the gift of my children.

In his short life, we found the most joyous moments together, and I thank God that I could be a part of Dee's life. He was so loving and completely selfless. He found happiness in the simplest things, nature, animals, family, everything simple, so beautiful. He was empathic, sensitive, humble, and compassionate, and he loved every person, every living creature, unconditionally.

Before I tell you about my reading, I want you to know my wonderful son. For you to really get a feeling for who he was and is. Dee had a big heroic heart. My son was driving on the highway. He saw a car pulled over and burst into flames. He immediately pulled over and jumped out of his truck. Dimitri saw an elderly man in the driver's seat and tried to get him out. The door would not open, so he grabbed a hammer from his tools in the back of the truck, broke the window, and opened it. Dee pulled the man out. He laid him on the grass, called 911, and waited for the first responders.

Another time, my son saw a homeless man walking with no coat, he took off his jacket and put it around the man's shoulders. The guy said, "Hey, man, I don't want to take your jacket!" My son said, "That's okay, where I'm going, I'll be nice and warm, don't worry, I have another one. You need it more than me, right now."

There are so many experiences that I can recall. My son was the most selfless, loving person I've ever met.

He is, without a doubt, my soulmate. We were so similar in so many ways. He was the youngest of my three children and my only son. I always told him that he was my favorite thing in the whole world, right under Jesus. When he died, a part of me died too.

In my reading, Allison mentioned to me that Dee said to her, "I always told him he was my favorite."

As a disclaimer, I love all of my children. He was, in fact, easy to love, it's true. During my reading with Allison, she said so many things that were profoundly meaningful to me.

She told me that my son heard me when I spoke to him very soon after his death. She told me that my son felt me touch his hand, he said, he was comforted by my touch and by my words. She asked me if I "held his hand right after he was deceased?"

I had talked to him and held his hand, in his room, right after he died. While his body and soul were still in the same place, in his bedroom, where I had found him, that terrible morning.

She said, that at the time of his passing, he felt confused, hazy and asked, if there was a medication of some sort, in his blood-stream.

I felt very confused when I found him in his room. When I saw my son, he looked pristine, in his white T-shirt and black shorts. His black Brooklyn baseball cap was placed backward on his head. He was sitting on the foot of his bed, resting his head on his dresser. He had died a Fentanyl related death.

Allison asked me, "did he make it past 17?" He had suffered a fatal overdose at 17. It was a crossing point for Dee, the first half of the year, wonderful, the second half, woeful. She told me that he wanted me to think of him when he was 17 before things got complicated. She conveyed that he said, he liked his hair back then.

I chimed in, "Yes, he did!"

She mentioned his grandfather being with him and how close their relationship was. My father had died 6 months before my son. I was happy to hear they were together.

She asked me, "Is there a military connection with the grand-father?"

He was a colonel in the army. He took my children to the

army base all the time, to the officers club, to the pool, so many happy days they spent together.

She said, she could see Dee and my father sitting at the kitchen table.

She said, "it is not a table like we have today, but a nostalgic table." I have an antique table in my kitchen that we have sat around many times.

Allison mentioned my son's favorite song, "Free Bird" by Lynyrd Skynyrd.

She continued, "the music he's playing is really an older song, for someone so young," My son was playing it for her in her head. He loved classic rock, and that was his favorite song!

Allison said, "people are going to get tattoos for him and that he would be sitting next to them snickering." No doubt, he would be.

Soon after my reading, my daughter went for one such tattoo. She was telling her tattoo artist about the reading and about how Allison had mentioned Free Bird and had explained how Dimitri reaches us through music. As she spoke, the song "Free Bird" came on over the speakers, and she knew immediately that he was there egging her on. I got a tattoo as well, on the first Mother's Day after his death. It was one of his own pieces of art that he had made for me.

Allison mentioned one of his favorite movies, Saturday Night Fever. Everyone used to compare Dee to Tony, the main character, played by John Travolta.

She said that he still likes to "sit on the couch and watch movies with a bowl of cereal."

He did indeed love to do that, and we watched movies all the time! He was a big movie buff. He could memorize scenes involving multiple characters and perform them for everyone. Cereal? Yes, it was one of his favorite snacks. He'd sit there with a giant bowl in his hands, describing movie scenes in between bites! Allison mentioned that my boy was talking about "Lucky Charms cereal."

It was his absolute favorite!

I remember the morning he died like it was yesterday. As I laid my hand on the banister, I felt as if he had passed. I came downstairs feeling strange, wondering if he was still in his room or had even come home? I remember thinking, as I looked toward the kitchen door, "I'll know he's okay if I see a bowl with bits of Lucky Charms in the sink." That morning, there wasn't. I was instantly worried.

She said, "your son liked the birthday party and says, 'thanks, mom!'" Allison asked me if I gave him a birthday party after he died?

I replied, yes. I had.

She mentioned his sense of humor and his cheeky personality. He was always telling us jokes, making people laugh, performing parodies and imitations. Her description of him was accurate.

Allison said, "I can see him playing cards." He loved to play cards, especially casino. She said that there were a lot of smokers in the family. That he was sitting in like a smoking section. Yes, he smoked, his sisters used to smoke, his girlfriend smokes, and his father smokes, so this made sense. Sometimes, when I smell smoke now, I know that he's around me.

She mentioned him liking his image on the computer screen. She described it as "big or large like a screensaver." His image was, in fact, my screensaver. My favorite picture of my son was on a large screen on my desktop computer.

She mentioned, my son's cell phone and how he likes it and how it's still on; he sees me look at it.

I still have it on, and his Facebook is still active. Every once in a while, family and friends send him a text or leave him a message. Sometimes, when his old friends message him on Facebook, I invite them over, sharing stories over dinner. I give them things that I know he would want them to have. The tales of his heartwarming acts of kindness toward others are endless, and I love hearing new ones. His friends brought me some of his artwork and photos that I'd never seen before, and in a way, it's like seeing him again.

Allison said, "he was a mama's boy... in a good way!" He was. Dee was always helpful, offering me rides to work, bringing me coffee, fixing things around the house, gardening, decorating, etc. She said he was my "buddy" from the time he was born. "You know," she said, "you just clicked!"

He was my buddy, my best buddy. No one could have said it better. We absolutely "clicked."

As Allison began wrapping up the reading, she closed, saying that my son said, "he's sorry." The night he died, he said, "he was impulsive and that he's so sorry, but that we can't change it now."

He did make a fateful decision that night, it was impulsive, I'm sure that he is sorry.

Dimitri suffered from depression, and he was a recovering drug addict, a dangerous combination. He doesn't suffer from it anymore, he's with his grandfather in spirit, and he's with me every day.

My Take on Melissa's Reading

As a mother myself, the thought of losing a child is unthinkable. As a medium, I see it all the time. Opioids are a huge problem in America, it's not someone else's problem anymore. I have brought through far too many sons in the past two years, who've died from overdoses. Decent kids, kind-hearted, sometimes they only took it once, and it robbed them of their life. Some pills say *Vicodin* on them, and they're actually *Fentanyl*. These poisonous pills pour over our southern border. They're sent from China, and they kill people. I hope that Melissa sharing her story with you might save a life. This is a preventable death, prescription drugs should only be taken when prescribed by doctors. Even then, you need to do your research to see what you're taking. Maybe even choosing a safer alternative. Teach your kids that they can die from taking one tainted pill given to them by a friend, who doesn't think it can hurt anyone. I brought a son through this year who took a tablet he thought was Vicodin with several of his best friends one weekend night, and they all died.

Dimitri came through so effortlessly fueled by the love he has for his mother. He seemed happy but apologetic, eager to share messages with his mom.

Melissa's son, Dimitri, had his whole life ahead of him. He was a fantastic guy that any of us would be lucky to know. I'm glad that Dee was able to make his mom laugh. Dee showed her that he's still part of his mom's life. He's still her son, he still loves her. Throughout the reading, I could feel their tight bond and their immeasurable love for one another. They're very cool soulmates, "partners in crime."

Dimitri will guide his mother, helping her navigate her daily life. Until the day comes when he helps her to crossover. I told Melissa, "Every day you wake up is a good day because it's a day closer to seeing your son again. He's not your past, you didn't leave him behind. He's your future, you're moving towards him."

Often that thought was the only thing that helped me get through each day after my dad died. Days after my dad passed, I was in church, railing at God for taking him. A voice whispered those sentences in my ear, and my perspective changed. I instantly felt calm. It made me feel better, the pain was still there, but its sting was less. I share this wisdom with my clients, hoping my words help them to heal, too.

GIFTS FROM ABOVE

SHERYL AND AJ

Sheryl

I was in a very dark place when I found out I was pregnant. I had left home at the age of 17, the daughter of teenage parents. I immediately enrolled in college but had basically been functioning as an adult since the age of 14. I was overwhelmed, then I fell into an emotionally abusive relationship with a man. He often had indiscretions with a bevy of other women. I just wanted someone to love me and take care of me, which he claimed, he was going to do. That was far from reality, and I ended up trying to take my own life.

When I found out that I was pregnant, it changed everything. I had a reason to live! My boyfriend tried to coerce me into an abortion. I refused, as this would be the first human being to have pure love for me. I struggled with a high-risk pregnancy that had multiple surprises. When the baby was emerging, the doctor said, "Looks like we have a little cleft here," and I immediately began to pray to God. How would my baby breathe? Eat? Live? "Why me?" I asked God. I didn't think I was prepared for this challenge; I was so uneducated. Then, they laid AJ on my chest.

"Hi! I'm your momma," I said. And the newborn's head whipped toward my voice. I was immediately in love. And that baby was the greatest blessing of my entire life.

I spent my life defending my son. When my boyfriend became my husband and tried to hold a pillow over our baby's head to quiet him, I threatened to kill my spouse. With the marriage over shortly after that incident, I became a single mom to AJ and his two younger sisters. It didn't matter, my little guy was the absolute light of my life. My daughters are the apples of my eye.

That was just the beginning of my defense of AJ. We lived in the rural suburbs of Des Moines, Iowa. AJ and his sisters were biracial, so they didn't fit-in. The cleft lip and cleft palate that AJ was born with made AJ different from most kids. I encouraged him and played his "cheerleader" when the kids got him down. My son and I were brought even closer through the shared experience of 16 surgeries- most of which occurred at the Shriner's Hospitals for Children in Chicago, Illinois. Just my boy and I; it was us against the world! I could barely tell that AJ had been born with the craniofacial birth defect, by the time he had completed those surgeries. Others were quick to notice that his nose wasn't perfectly straight, he had a scar on his lips, and his voice had a small lisp.

However, the straw that would break the camel's back for AJ was something else, he had no choice in his sexuality. From the time he was a toddler, I thought that he was gay; he loved playing dress-up, caring for babies, and had a very effeminate nature. Even though AJ was unique from his femininity, and the scars from his surgeries, I thought it was his differences that made him so beautiful. He was highly emotionally intelligent. Like me, he was an empath, he felt for others. He was my baby, my *person,* the individual that drove everything that I did. The human being that made me "Mom." He was the first person I thought of, with every decision I made. It's not that I love my daughters less, because I don't, it was just a different relationship. I couldn't describe the strong pull I had to my son; the connection was divine.

Ultimately, AJ was outed at his high school. He embraced his sexuality, but his peers took issue with it. AJ was relentlessly bullied by kids, staff, and administration because he was flamboyant. My son ended up being the 14th suicide in a decade at his school. He was the kindest person I have ever known. I immediately began making plans to end my own life when AJ was declared dead at the hospital.

My AJ had other plans. Despite a decade of failed in vitro attempts and my tubes being tied for 13 years, I found out I was pregnant, just days after burying my son. I lost my only son and had another, in less than eight months, 17 years apart! AJ's namesake, my miracle baby, is so much like my angel, that it sometimes hurts. Yet, my miracle baby couldn't drag me out of the throes of depression, nothing could. I felt lost in this world without my son. I had to go in-patient at a mental health Center. Despite the baby and my daughters, I was struggling to find purpose in life.

I went into menopause, went on a bunch of antidepressants, and began to simply exist. Then, after several years without ovulating, I started having some bizarre menopause symptoms. Only to find out that I was half-way through pregnancy, with miracle baby #2. My fifth baby, and third son, was finally enough to make me want to live again.

That said, I regularly struggle with the thought of being here without my firstborn. I cannot wait to be with AJ again. I feel so alone. Like part of my heart is missing, part of me is missing! While I won't be doing anything to get myself to heaven sooner, I cannot wait to be reunited with him. I love my other four children, fiercely. I just cannot help feeling that I am missing a huge part of me. I pray for peace every day, as it has been nearly seven years, and it never gets easier.

SHERYL'S TAKE ON OUR READING

AJ has done an excellent job of leaving me dimes to let me know that he is with me. Allison referenced the dimes in my reading. I asked AJ to give me a sign that she was talking to him. Less than 30 minutes later, I found a dime in the clothes dryer with my toddler's clothes; it was just sitting on the edge, right in front of my face. Message received, AJ!

Allison then said, "AJ likes to play with your lights as a sign that he's around you. He likes to send signs that he's there through electricity."

Sometimes for weeks at a time, AJ will illuminate the light inside my china hutch, where I have his memorial. The only way to turn the light on in the hutch is to touch a hinge, that is high of-f-the-ground. My husband certainly doesn't bother himself with it; the babies cannot reach it. Yet, on as bright as possible each morning, there it is when I come downstairs. It helps me to know that my baby boy is still here with me, in my home. I may not be able to see him, smell him, or hear him, yet I sense he is here.

In my reading, Allison said something that no naysayer could ever deny is a sign of my son's presence. Right before my phone reading was about to start, "Miracle Baby #1" asked why I don't have a photo in one of the picture frames on my desk. I just haven't been focused on putting photographs in frames, since AJ died. So, my five-year-old and I picked-out a photo that we loved of AJ. After everyone left my home for the day, I began printing-off pictures to put in an odd-shaped picture frame. It took a couple of times to get the size right. Allison called for my reading and asked, "Did you have to print a photo of AJ several times to fit it in a frame?"

I began to cry, AFFIRMATION of my son's presence, beside me! I immediately clutched the heart locket around my neck, which says my son's name, birth date, and death date; it has his photo inside. I held the locket tight, placed it inside of my shirt, and held it against my heart.

Allison then asked, "Do you have a locket, that you wear for AJ?"

When I affirmed that I did and that I was holding it, Allison said she knew. Allison indicated that "AJ is standing next to you and he saw you grab the locket and place it near your heart."

Allison has blessed me immeasurably. I can continue living in this world, until the day I see my soulmate again. Allison was able to provide me with communication, with my son, I'm at ease. God bless her. I don't know what I would do without her.

My Take on Sheryl's Reading

You'd never know that Sheryl has been through so much in her life because of her sunny disposition. She shared her story with you, and I'm sure you'd agree, Sheryl's been to hell and back. I found the level of honesty she shared regarding her life to be very raw and a reflection of her desire to help others to move through their own pain. AJ was unlike some of the other stories shared in this chapter. He hadn't felt like he belonged in the living world for a long time. It wasn't one moment of depression mixed with alcohol or drugs. He preluded to there being no contentment for him on earth, "he couldn't stay."

Some souls are not wired for the ugliness we face in the real world. Their soul is too sensitive, too gentle, to be here.

AJ had happy days in his life, but he referred to many of the good memories, taking place when he was still small. I see this a lot in readings with textbook suicides. AJ said, "I am with grandpa and I am a young child of 5 or 6 years old."

Sheryl told me that's how old AJ was when she married her husband. That's when her father in law, became AJ's grandfather. AJ spoke of "rainbows are a sign" and talked about his love of Hawaii. His mother confirmed he did love Hawaii, and the family had just traveled there. He was letting her know that he went too. He showed me the number '17', Sheryl said she had '17' tattooed on her after AJ died. He said he would've ended up on stage.

Sheryl shared that he had aspired to be on Broadway someday. He wiped a tear from his eye. When I shared this with Sheryl, she had apparently done this in tandem with him. I explained that he feels what she feels. AJ spoke a lot about his siblings and how much he loves them. He talked about playing in his oldest sister's clothes. He followed that with, "Tell her not to let herself go!"

He was playing with her, this statement was an attempt to make his sister laugh. Spirits interact with us, they try and force a smile on our face or make us laugh. They want to still be part of the family dynamic.

AJ felt content to me, centered and sure of himself. He enjoys being around his family, both the living and the ones who "live again." He didn't want to play the game of life anymore, but his love for his family was enduring and lives within him. Sheryl was sent two miracle babies after her son died, sent by a force bigger than us, to save her. The people we love can't be replaced, but we are often sent other people to give us life. To resuscitate us back to the living world. We will all lose the people we love most, some of us will be the ones others cry for, ache to see again. That's the physical world. In the Spirit World, we are restored, reunited with those we lost. But, our "heaven" isn't complete until we have everyone we love with us. Savor, life feeling good, revel in your good fortune, to feel so incredibly happy.

As we get older, we stop receiving as many gifts, and instead, they are taken away; that's life. Your happiest days on earth will become your heaven, so bask in the light! Be a glutton for life, love with everything you've got, and don't live in a prison of guilt and apology. Life is what you make it, we're all thrown curveballs, it's how you recover from being thrown off balance that defines who you are and how you choose to spend your time on earth. Sheryl will be with AJ again someday. Until then, I hope she fills her days with as much joy and excitement as possible. I understand that life is less beautiful without the ones we love, but the world still holds beauty for us to collect.

My Girl

Aurora and Hailey

Aurora

When someone you love suddenly dies, it feels similar in a way to skydiving. You watch people jump out the door of an airplane, and they evaporate, somewhere into the sky. You can't see them anywhere, just a poof in the wind, and they are gone. You land on the ground and run towards each other, full of adrenaline, high fives, and endless smiles. When someone you love dies without warning, there is no one waiting on the ground. They simply evaporate.

I am a mom of all boys, and my niece, Hailey, was my girl. My sister had only one child, a daughter, who really became "our" daughter. Hailey knew the struggles I have had, that my son has had, and most importantly, she knew with me, she would never, ever, be judged. Hailey and I were amazingly alike. We loved to zip line, ski the black diamonds, and kayak with the whales! No girly, girls here. We wanted to fully live life and eat a lot of sushi!

My sister called me late on March 19, 2019, around 10 p.m.

California time, and midnight, Texas time. She and I didn't talk much, so I answered the phone, thinking it was probably some form of family drama. I never in a million years, expected to hear the words, "Hailey shot herself in the head and died."

It's true what they say when you get news like this, you collapse to the floor, and a sound emits from your mouth that is unlike any other human sound. Some describe it as the death howl, I guess it is. Hailey was only 29 years old.

Theories were going around as to whether or not her death was a suicide or a murder. For about a year, Hailey's ex-boyfriend was relentless in making her life miserable. The day she died, she had been with a new guy. His story was that Hailey had the gun for protection. According to her friends, she had not been going to work, had been sleeping a lot, and she had asked to come to see me in California for a break. I told her that it might not be a good idea since she had already missed so much work. I feel terrible about that now. I had a gut feeling that something was not right. I knew she had been prescribed Xanax and Adderall, legally, and she was drinking a fair amount. She was a distributor for a liquor company. She already had her Bachelor's Degree and was working towards becoming a Physician's Assistant. The call with her request to visit me was the day before she died, and I specifically asked her if she was suicidal. She said no. The following day I tried frantically to get a hold of her, she was not responding. I planned on giving her some advice. She should leave Texas and make a new start somewhere else. Maybe with me, in California? Unfortunately, we never had that conversation.

People were confused, including me, as to whether this was a murder or a suicide. In part, because her relentless ex-boyfriend, died a few months after her, of an apparent drug overdose. People had suspected it may have been a guilt-induced purposeful overdose if he indeed killed Hailey.

According to law enforcement and the Medical Examiner, there was no question in their minds; this was a suicide. I was supposed to accept their conclusions. However, there is that lingering doubt that creeps up in your mind. Was it?

I sure wished it had been a murder and not a suicide. It's hard to reconcile that our Hailey would willingly leave us. To this day, her mother believes it was a murder. Knowing she was in such pain troubles me terribly, to this day.

About four months had passed, I was watching an old Oprah Winfrey show rerun from years ago. I had never heard of Allison DuBois, or the television show Medium. However, I saw Allison on the Oprah show, and I was intrigued by her involvement with law enforcement, unsolved crimes, and how she amazed the guests on the Oprah show. I had never been to a psychic or medium before.

I googled the name Allison DuBois and randomly sent an email to inquire about a private reading. I wanted to know what the hell happened to our Hailey? I booked my appointment and met with her a few months later in Scottsdale, not knowing what to expect.

The first thing she said was, "She's telling me you're the funny Aunt, the fun Aunt, who is more like a mother to her than her own mom."

And from there, I was sort of shell shocked into the details that Allison knew. Allison saw Hailey's beloved french bulldog, Duke, who now lives with me. She said, "I know it sounds juvenile, but I hear the song 'I Hope you Dance' by Leanne Womack in my head." That was the last song played at Hailey's memorial. Allison described precisely what I thought, the police thought, and Hailey's friends thought, a term none of us had heard before: Accidental Suicide. When she brought Hailey thru, she said, "I feel foggy, not clear, like something was in her system." Allison said, "I gotta tell ya, she glows, and she loved life. She didn't mean to go."

She loved life, Hailey loved life. She was beautiful with her long blonde hair and bright blue eyes. She did glow. This was good and bad, right? Good that it was an "accident," something she never would have done if it wasn't for the drugs and alcohol. Bad, because it was an "accident" that never should have happened. Mainly, Allison brought about peace for our family and friends. There was no doubt in my mind, Allison connected with Hailey. When I played the recording of our time together for my family and friends, everyone had a little more peace and a lot less skepticism. I have always had an unwavering belief system, believing in a loving God, a Universal God. However, it all becomes much more apparent when a complete stranger can know what Allison knew.

As if the reading with Allison were not enough, the following month was definitely astounding. Allison said, "Hailey will connect with me thru songs." While I was in the shower one morning, the song "See You Again" by Carrie Underwood downloaded ITSELF to my phone (no record of a transaction and payment charge). I live in Silicon Valley, with maybe one Country music station, Carrie Underwood, was nowhere on my radar. I had never heard the song before.

Another little miracle was that a picture of Hailey and I popped up on my iPhone home setting one night while I was sleeping. Not just on my phone, but a picture of my son and Hailey popped up on his phone, and also one of my sister and Hailey on her iPhone. We all had these supernatural screenshots divinely sent to us within days of each other. Thank God for screenshots! There were a few other little signs from the Otherside. Most importantly, I know in my soul that she's okay.

My reading with Allison brought so many of us who loved Hailey the a-okay to believe that what we were seeing or hearing really is, her. She's still with us, just in a different form. I know she loved life and loves me. And I also know, I will "See You Again."

My Take on Aurora's Reading

Aurora's reading was an example of the times we live in right now. When Hailey came through, she talked about her aunt being a "second mother to her." She seemed to really love her graduation picture in her cap and gown. She kept referring to that time in her life as being full of hope and excitement. She said she got her aunt's "social butterfly" gene. When we got into how she died, she talked about "being around the wrong people." She said, "I tried to fix people, I gave them the benefit of the doubt."

Hailey said that she felt "numb, and her head was foggy when she died." That's what dead people say who had drugs or alcohol in their system. She mentioned, "The person who was there, didn't do enough for her. He was afraid, he placed a phone call before getting her help."

I know that it sounds strange to people when I say, "It was an accident." If someone shoots themselves, how can I say, "It was an accident."? If they have drugs and/or alcohol in their system when it happens, their brain chemistry is off. The imbalance can contribute to the violent act of taking one's life; therefore, some wouldn't have killed themselves if they were sober. They likely didn't know that the mixing of chemicals would end their life. They may have wanted a temporary escape from life's stress. So, when their mind went to dark places they didn't intend to go to, the dead feel the chemicals were in control, not them. The chemicals pulled the trigger. Now, this isn't all suicides, many young people hadn't felt they belonged here since early childhood. Even their mother saw the depression and signs of suicide surface when their child was small. To the child, the world didn't feel like a place where they belonged, and they didn't want to be here. I see far too much medicating of young people.

When they're medicated in childhood, it has to affect their brain chemistry and how their brain forms. Also, young people are growing up thinking there's a pill to cure whatever ails you. Every other commercial on television is selling a quick fix to what ails you. When you listen to the prescription drugs' side effects, they often sound more severe than the issue you're trying to improve. When Generation X and generations before them were growing up, there were no drug commercials, other than headache or cold medicine. So, it was easier to distinguish who was suicidal. Kids might smoke a joint and drink a beer, but nothing hardcore like we have now.

I'm seeing far too many young people die because they thought Adderall or Xanax would make everything better. The drugs might help some, but in my opinion, young people are being overprescribed. When they're of drinking age, alcohol gets introduced into their social lives, and that's what I call a perfect storm. They're still taking the pills, but now, they're knocking the pills back with alcohol. It's like the red pills and blue pills of the 1970s, uppers, and downers, except now they're more accessible and freely prescribed by doctors. So, young people have a false sense of security, thinking they're safe. The human brain is a complicated center to have. A chemical change can affect how a person feels, thinks, and weighs consequences. Hailey seemed to be a young woman who sometimes used pills to cope with life in general. On the night that she died, they got the best of her. If Hailey wanted to die that night, couldn't she just take a handful of Xanax if she wanted to end it? Hailey didn't start out the night, wanting to die. The toxic combination of chemicals likely ushered in dark thoughts. Ultimately, leading to Hailey's death.

Hailey and her Aunt had a strong bond. They had a real soul connection. You feel more alive when you're with a soulmate like Hailey, and Aurora did jumping out of airplanes and whale watching together. Nobody else even comes close to giving you life the way a soulmate does. You find greater comfort being with them more than anyone else on earth. Many people feel like they've met someone they love now, in another time, in another place. I would say that it's possible they have been together, loved one another before. The relationship of who they are to one another may be different, through time. The original connection could remain deeply embedded inside of them in the deepest recesses of their soul. Love cannot be destroyed nor extracted; it remains, searching for its match again. Hailey saw Aurora as a "second mom." Aurora saw her niece, as no different than her own daughter. If souls live many lifetimes, is it possible that they were mother and daughter in another time? People who believe in Soulmates and some physicists would say, it's possible.

Either way, the bond that Aurora and Hailey share will not diminish over time. It will remain. Hailey will watch over Aurora until the day, that Aurora finds herself joining Hailey, beyond the veil.

I WALK THE LINE

KAREN AND PJ

Karen

Our son, Philip (PJ) Waisman, died July 22, 2018. He was not only a son, but he was also a brother, a grandson, and a friend to many. He has a beautiful soul that lives on in me. He was kind, warm, loving, generous, and only wanted to help others. He was very actively involved in Boy Scouts, from a Cub Scout all the way to a Life Scout. He was on the skiing/mountain climbing team and marching band all through high school. He loved to be active and hike, go camping or hang out with his mom, dad, and two sisters. We were always a spontaneous family. He loved exploring new areas with us, whether it was on a Disney cruise to Mexico or a trip to Washington, D.C. My son had many friends, was working part-time, and looking forward to college plans. He had a brilliant mind and was accepted to the University of North Carolina, Asheville. We were so proud and so happy for him.

When he found out he would have to live on campus for the first year, he suddenly no longer cared to attend. He suffered from depression and social anxiety. We begrudgingly accepted his decision, knowing that one day he would attend college when he was ready.

After PJ graduated high school, all of his friends went to college. My son sank into a depression. He became obsessed with video games, not wanting to leave his room or join us when we went out. This is the same boy that had walked his shy little sister to class every day in second grade because he knew she was afraid. He had taken her under his wing when she was a Freshman, and he was a Senior in high school. He introduced her to all his friends. He was popular with his bandmates and made sure his sister became one of the crowd. How could this be the same guy who was a huge Star Wars fan who was surprised by a trip to MGM for Star Wars Day in May by his parents? With eyes as big as saucers, he looked at his dad and me and exclaimed that "this is the best day ever!"

He had disappeared.

I was concerned about his depression and his withdrawal from us. I went to drastic measures. I had my son admitted to a psych hospital for the treatment of depression. I took him to the doctors and to therapy for a few months. One day, he said he no longer wanted to go back to treatment. The doctors put him on antidepressants. After a few weeks, he refused to take them, stating, "I don't want to put any more chemicals in my body."

He was an adult at this point, I could not force him to take the medication. He even told me that if I planned on admitting him to a psych hospital again, not to bother, he knew exactly what to say, to get released.

I have been a registered nurse for sixteen years, and I know the signs of depression and suicide. At this point, my husband and I were travel nursing. We went home every week. The first thing I would do was check him for signs of worsening depression or suicidal idealization. In June 2018, my son and I talked. PJ told me he thought he was drinking too much and wanted to quit. I was with him when he stopped drinking, and I told him the signs and symptoms to look for with detox; to call me if he noticed these symptoms. PJ said he wanted to change his lifestyle; he started working out, hiking again, eating healthier, and found himself a job that he liked. People treated him with respect. He was the happiest we had seen him in four years. Roughly two weeks later, he came to me and told me that he wanted to quit smoking. He said it was worse than quitting drinking. He was anxious, agitated, and couldn't concentrate. We found his antidepressants that he had discarded, and he started retaking them. He said he had not felt that good in years, and could I get him scheduled with his doctor? I told him he had to do it, but I would happily go with him if he wanted me to go. He had skipped the appointments that I had made for him in the past. He said he would. We were all happy with the changes he was making, he was making an effort to change his life. He had told me that his youngest sister, whom he had always been close to, "no longer liked him."

I said, "She loves you. If you want to reestablish a relationship with her, offer to help her with demolition on her boyfriend's house."

He came, and we all had a great time. I thought things were finally back on track for him. Who would quit smoking and drinking, if they had plans to end their life? I was so proud of how hard he was trying.

On the night of July 22, 2018, our lives changed forever. His girlfriend had broken up with him; he asked if they could remain friends? She replied back, "No" That was all the push it took for him to make a rash decision. Less than 30 minutes later, he was gone. PJ killed himself after drinking some alcohol. My world was shattered; this was my firstborn, my only son, my love, my life. I could no longer embrace life, as I once had.

I needed to hear from him, as I am lost without him on earth. I contacted Allison DuBois and set up a reading. The date was February 5, 2020, a year and a half after he passed.

I was so nervous. Allison understood that and told me, "I was doing great."

My son came through, and the very first message was that he was "numb" when he died and did not feel pain.

This had been a significant concern for me, as I did not want him to suffer. The next message Allison said was, "Nothing would have saved him; he was in a very dark place and made a hasty decision that he wished he could take back."

The guilt I have carried for not being there that night has eaten me alive. I have fallen into a deep depression and the what-ifs? Are what my nightmares are made of. The third message was, "Yes, he knows how much we all love him and especially how much I love him."

No matter how many people tell me that there was nothing I could do to save my boy, hearing it from my son himself finally started the healing process. The absolutely ironic thing is, these were the first three questions I had written down for her to ask him. Except, I hadn't told her what they were yet, he answered my questions without being asked. She gave us a message that "His sister will get her trip down the aisle and no more tattoos!"

This was in regards to his middle sister. Her wedding was scheduled for April of this year. She had recently broken up with her fiance and does indeed have too many tattoos! Allison mentioned that "PJ was with a man named James from my husband's side."

He was with Uncle Jimmy, he had passed away while I was pregnant with PJ. He also said, "He was with my grandmother, who was like a mother to me," Grammy Rose. She passed away before his first birthday. He told Allison that, "I had to let the grief out and I needed to stop wishing, I was with him, he was with me every day holding my hand."

Allison said that PJ told her that, "You have to get rid of the barrier that you have unintentionally put up between your husband and yourself."

He said, "Dad is grieving, just differently from me, and he knows that Dad would have given his life for him."

Allison had no idea that the messages she passed through to our family, and I would have such a profound effect on us all. I feel lighter, still grieving, but no longer feeling like I let my son down. I know that my son is being cared for by our family. He did not suffer when he died. It soothes me, knowing that PJ feels our love for him. To hear that he is not alone; has brought me more comfort than I had ever hoped to achieve. Thank you, Allison, for helping us to heal.

My Take on Karen's Reading

PJ came through and said, he reverted to being '17' again; that's what he looks like now. He talked about his birthday, and he showed me a birthday cake and thanked his mom for his birthday party. She acknowledged that the family had indeed had a birthday party for him after he died. PJ then showed me himself sitting in a truck with the window rolled down and a big grin on his face. He mentioned he liked driving, he "likes road trips." His mother, Karen, confirmed the vehicle. PJ held a black puppy next to his face and nuzzled it. He wanted his mom to know that their dog was with him, she confirmed they had black labs. One had died, he had it with him on the Otherside. Like people, often, dogs, cats, horses you name it, will revert to a younger age when they die. His dog was a puppy again.

He was very proud of being a "free spirit like mom." He liked that his mom was strong, but also that she was not afraid to take chances. PJ said, "I feel guilty about how I died. I wasn't in control of myself." PJ elaborated, saying, "My head wasn't right. I'm young, I made a mistake. But, mom, you can't be with me, you have work to do."

I feel for Karen, she did everything she could to keep her son healthy and safe. Even a mother's love is often not enough to protect children from themselves. PJ would have to be affected by quitting smoking and drinking at the same time. He was having trouble coping with life, and those were his two emotional crutches; drinking and smoking. The physical withdrawals must have been tough on his psyche too. When his relationship abruptly ended, I don't feel he had the strength to cope with the pain. He already had a hard time dealing with life. I don't blame the ex-girlfriend. Relationships end all the time. She's going to have to live with thinking she's somewhat responsible for PJ's death. She's not, though. I know that PJ wouldn't want anyone to blame her; he'd take responsibility for his impulsive decision. Sometimes it's easier if we have a villain.

I do a lot of readings, and it's prevalent with suicides that a break-up precipitated the death. Often, the ex-relationship is blamed, but they're just the straw that broke the weary camel's back. There were pre-existing problems that were factors in the death, too. Honestly, life is a lot to cope with, everyone stumbles from time to time. Some people are better equipped to navigate life than others. PJ was very loved and quite lost at the time that he died. He may have been able to get past getting over the break-up, my sense is that he would have. He didn't feel like someone who was always suicidal. He had a chemical imbalance. Sometimes it's hard to find the right combination of medications, to bring balance to your mind and body, making it possible to cope with setbacks.

I pray that PJ can shelter his mom's heart from pain and visits her often.

THIRD TIMES THE CHARM

MONICA AND KENNY

Monica

Kenny was not supposed to be born, I had a tough pregnancy.

His dad and I prayed and prayed, and we were blessed with our third son. He was a healthy baby boy, born full term. Since he was a scheduled c-section, we were able to pick his birthday. We chose January 23rd, 1/23. We thought when we were very old, and forgetfulness a part of our makeup, we would be able to re-call the numbers 1-2-3. Little did we know...

Kenny seemed to have a special relationship with each member of the family. He was everyone's soulmate. Kenny was his dad's little buddy. He followed his dad everywhere from the time Kenny could walk to the year he died. If anything needed fixing in the house, he was right by his dad's side helping him. Kenny followed his dad's footsteps into accounting.

He enjoyed anything outdoorsy, with his oldest brother Shawn. They hiked together and had plans for several more hikes, in addition to rock climbing. There was an occasion when Shawn was not able to continue the walk carrying his equipment. Kenny took Shawn's equipment and his own, telling him, "We can do this!"

With his brother Eric, he shared a love of sports. Both played ice hockey. Both had a lot of friends with like interests, they also enjoyed a good party. Six months to the day of Kenny's death, he was supposed to be Eric's best man at his wedding, and I have no doubt that he would have been asked to be Shawn's best man too. He was very close to both of his brothers.

Kenny was my fellow Aquarian. He had a very easy-going temperament. There were times that I felt I could communicate with him without using words. It was the strangest feeling. We just seemed to know what the other wanted. He was my fashionista. Being the mom of three boys, you don't get to spend much time shopping, but Kenny was always up for a trip to the mall. He loved shopping, he was a great bargain hunter. And like his mom, he never shopped without a coupon in hand.

Kenny was so very bright. He graduated from college in five years, with a master's degree in accounting and a dual undergraduate degree in Finance and Accounting. Before his death, my son was studying for the last portion of the CPA exam. He had a great first job. We knew he would be moving on from there to bigger and better things. The sky was the limit! He made a mistake one night and hit a pole to avoid hitting a deer. His car was totaled, and he got a DUI. That was Thursday night. Saturday afternoon, we were notified by the police that our son had died by suicide.

What gave me comfort from Allison's reading was that she said he was not a depressed spirit. He did not feel typical of someone who had taken their own life. You see, I always felt that. I knew our son died in that car accident. I always felt that Kenny had a head injury from the accident that affected his judgment center. Allison said he was not entirely coherent. He did not know what he was doing, and he did not think of the consequences. When a parent loses a child by suicide, you question everything. What did I miss? How could I not see this level of depression? Allison said to me that he does not feel suicidal, not your kid. He is not and was not depressed. Allison told me Kenny said, "there was nothing anyone could have done that would have changed the outcome."

He made a rash decision that was life-ending. Knowing this does make it a bit easier. Every day forward is a day closer to being together again.

MY TAKE MONICA'S ON READING

Kenny came through quickly and was happy to talk to his mom. He said he went back to being 16 again when his mom babied him still, and he liked it.

He said, "My mom is the best mom in the whole world."

He mentioned being around "Rose" and said, "She's a hoot!"

Monica said she had an Aunt Rose and that she was hilarious.

He talked about sending his mom, "emotionally triggering songs in the car when he rides with her."

Monica said, "I feel Kenny in the car, and he does send me emotionally triggering songs."

He then said, "Birthday Buddies!"

Meaning that Kenny shares the time around his birthday with another family member. Monica said, "Our birthdays are close together."

He was acknowledging their closeness and his need for her birthday to be a happy day, his too. Not sad and painful, with his mom holding her breath until they pass. He wanted them both to be celebrated, he liked having their birthdays side by side. Kenny then talked about a dog that's a "Retriever." I asked Monica, "Do you have Retrievers who've passed?"

"He is also talking about retrievers who can sense when he's there, and they react."

She said, "We have retrievers both living and who've passed."

Kenny showed one dog in particular with him, that had light hair. Monica said, "We had a white one named Lily."

Lily, is Kenny's companion now, in spirit, and the living dogs know when Kenny's around the house. Her son talked about many details of his life and his family's lives, which is typical in readings. What I found that stood out was his energy in the first part of the reading, in contrast with how he felt to me around his time of death. They seemed like two very different energies.

He said things that didn't exactly fit with suicide. I couldn't put my finger on why? Later on in the reading, Monica mentioned that Kenny had sustained a head injury, not long before his death. This detail was actually a big deal. The brain is a very complicated part of us, so powerful, yet so fragile. Kenny didn't *feel* to me like he had earlier in the reading. When he talked about the moments leading up to his death, he made my head feel hazy and confused. When I tapped into his energy, it didn't feel quite like Kenny. Earlier in the reading, he felt so full of life and light-hearted. He loved his family more than anything, and he seemed excited about life in general. In the moments leading up to his death, he felt extremely depressed to me, useless, emotionally unattached to other people. Unlike the young man, I had tapped into at the beginning of the reading. They seemed like two different people. I asked Monica, "If the medical examiner had been able to check for abnormalities or brain injuries, in the autopsy?"

She told me that due to how Kenny died, they were unable to check him for prior injuries. I shared with Monica my sense was that Kenny had a head injury that affected his ability to weigh consequences or think clearly."

She said that in the car accident, "his frontal lobe had been impacted when he hit the pole, which affects his *judgment*."

But for his earlier car accident, I don't believe Kenny's life would have ended in the manner that it did. His inability to weigh consequences and exercise good judgment would have a direct correlation to his suicide. I've read over 10,000 people, and this reading is unusual. Since his mother is in the medical field, she understood the effects of brain injuries. For me, experiencing the contrast between Kenny's original energy compared to his around his time of death was a teaching moment. He went from being vibrant, youthful energy to a confused, low-frequency leading up to his death. Then, he was restored to his original state after death. I'm relieved that he's once again full of joy, love, and contentment, but I feel deeply for his family, who miss him daily. I hope in some small way, I helped the family to better understand that their son/brother did love life and just wasn't himself when he exited this world.

Kenny said, "I know how much they all love me, and I still want to be part of the family."

I have no doubt that the people who love him will continue to have warm thoughts of him, reflecting on the memories they share. He'll live in their hearts and minds until they see him again.

What does love mean to you?

_____

_____

_____

_____

_____

_____

Medium: Joe's Not Dead

There's a handful of people who are lucky enough to inspire a television show or a movie. I was fortunate enough to be one of them. I heard from a lot of fans (still do) after the series finale of the television show based on my life, MEDIUM. They were none too happy about how the series ended. I can't say that I blame them, I wasn't particularly thrilled either. So, I wrote this chapter for fans of the show and for my fans, who often ask me, "Is Joe, alright?"

My husband Joe and I really began when we met at Gators (An Arizona State University, sports bar) in July 1992. I still remember the first moment that I laid eyes on him. He had a goofy smile on his young face, he was sitting down at a booth. I was standing in front of him, watching Chuck Hall's band play. He tugged on my skorts (that'll date me) to get my attention, and the rest is history.

We never could have imagined that our love story would lead to a hit television show. I was only 32 years old when the pilot episode of MEDIUM was filmed. I was pretty young, and to have a television show based on my life and to be thrown into that level of fame, made my head spin. I wasn't in the "industry" striving to be an actress or anything, where there's an understanding of what fame would be like. I was a housewife, a mother of three little girls. I had a degree in Political Science and History, and I was trying to make a difference in the world, to help prevent child abduction. I was in my late twenties. I had produced a safety video for kids to know "what to do" and "not to do" if ever approached by a stranger. I initiated the Amber Alert, for the state of Arizona and served on the Task Force, to design it. So, I had some experience on the local news, being interviewed, as a child abduction prevention expert, by the time MEDIUM aired. As for "real fame," worldwide fame, I had to learn that by trial and error. Nobody prepares you to be recognized around the world. I had people from Japan who saw me interviewed there, identify me on their vacation in Sydney, Australia. People recognized my voice in the grocery store, in Scottsdale, Arizona, from two aisles over and came to see if it was "really" me.

A little girl came to my door Trick or Treating on Halloween. She had a blonde clip in her bangs, she wore a little suit and carried a briefcase. I asked her, "who are you dressed up to look like?"

She responded, "Allison DuBois!"

My daughters had a good laugh over that one.

I wore sunglasses on flights, to avoid being probed for hours, should the person next to me, recognize me. I was seated in the first row on a plane going home to Phoenix. Ten minutes before landing, the woman next to me said, "You should read this book!

It's excellent." She turned the cover towards me, I was looking at myself, on the cover of my second book, *We Are Their Heaven*. I said, "I'll have to check it out."

When I was exiting the plane, she was taking down her bag, so her hands were full. I looked back at her, lowered my sunglasses, and said, "I'm thrilled you liked my book."

She replied, "If I'd known it was you, I would've had so many questions for you."

My response, "I know."

When I fly, and people ask what I do, I say, "I'm a secretary."

It's not a lie. I'm a "secretary to the dead."

That's what I tell my clients when they say they're nervous before a reading. I tell them, "You're the magic. You're why the dead come through. I'm just a secretary, I take down their messages and pass them on to you." That always seems to make my clients feel a bit better.

Being recognized with no make-up on and in sweatpants is the worst because your fan still wants a picture with you. I am not one of those natural beauties! So, losing your anonymity takes some getting used to. Don't get me wrong, fame has a lot of nice perks too! Once you get used to being stared at by strangers, the rest is pretty enjoyable.

7 SEASONS

Season 1, consisted of too many media interviews to count (Joe actually has them cataloged somewhere). Reporters wanted me to predict whether or not MEDIUM, would be a hit. Sometimes, it felt as though they were waiting for it to fail, so I'd be wrong. When it was a huge hit, debuting to more than 17 million viewers on the first night, headlines ran saying things like, "MEDIUM, RARE and WELL DONE."

The first season was a rush, a lot of traveling, a lot of change. Season 2, you could see people who worked on the show relax a little because we had been picked up for season 2, within weeks of our pilot debut. I traveled so much, on press tours and book tours, I had to go back and watch Season 2 years later. I was in so many different time zones, I missed that whole season. On the road, I learned that television hosts are almost all friendly people. Radio hosts are a toss of the coin. Some were really nice, very interested in life after death. Then, you have the jackasses, who liked to spend the segment ridiculing, life after death. I figured, everyone finds out for themselves eventually, so don't sweat it. That didn't make it any less annoying at the time to be patronized by men trying to be, shock jocks. I had an Australia radio host, say, "Isn't it true that you're just famous, because you're good looking?"

The young me reacted, offended, but you know, now that I'm older, I'm rather amused by his statement. Now, I'd say, "What a lovely thing to say, thank you!"

At the time, I had jumped through so many hoops to prove my abilities, from scientists, to live television readings. I was tired of being challenged; after a while, it gets old. Now, instead of having controls in place, to make sure a reading on air is legit, they edit and produce the segments on cable. It almost seems scripted. People just seem to take them at their word now. It wasn't like that in the early 2000s. My friend John Edward (Host of Crossing Over and medium extraordinaire), and I cleared many hurdles to further the public's understanding of mediumship and life after death. He and I have talked about our contributions in the spiritual realm, and we're very proud of ours.

It was fascinating to see how the television and publishing industries are around the world. I loved press tours in Japan! The people are the most humble, zen, energy I've ever encountered. Although learning Japanese on the fly for their television station breaks, wasn't easy. Australia is another favorite of mine! A true Aussie will quickly become one of your favorite people, they are upbeat, positive, and cheerful, they're also loyal. I have come away with several close Australian friends.

England was different, London, was not so friendly, to me. My television interviews were canceled last minute. There was a backlash taking place against American television. At the time, they felt that American television was more present there than British television. I got caught in the crosshairs.

My book signing in London was canceled a couple of hours before it was scheduled because the books didn't get there on time? Well, who's responsible for that? I was more upset that people were coming in on trains, wasting their time, for nothing. The people who arranged the signing didn't seem worried about inconveniencing my fans, that annoyed me further. I was on a radio show there, and the host said, "There's a note here that says, you don't want to talk about skeptics. Why is that?"

(So, Englishmen aren't all gentlemen.) My response was, "That's correct because the skeptics' topic takes up the limited air time we have, and we don't get to talk about what really matters; life after death. Skeptics make absolutely no difference in the world."

Honestly, they help no one. Skeptic's criticisms are based on ego, no understanding of the paranormal, and insults laced with disdain. So, I didn't find them relevant to talk about. London ended up being a bit of a letdown.

Seasons 3 through 5 were a blur to me; I was still touring and trying to balance my personal life with my professional life. The publishing industry began crumbling, as our economy tanked. Paramount and CBS merged, I asked Glenn Caron if that was a conflict of interest? (Since, CBS was in direct competition with NBC, our network). He wasn't worried; in Season 5, we were canceled by NBC and picked up by CBS on the same day. You be the judge. In season 6, we were still doing really well in the ratings on CBS when I was told that season 7 would be our last season. I was a little sad, but the child actors were getting older (along with my own daughters), so I understood. I felt so blessed to have inspired such a unique, powerfully written show. It opened a lot of people's minds, to the topic of life after death, and our ability to communicate with lost loved ones. It also lets young mediums know that they're part of a very cool club. That's why it's called a "gift."

In Season 7, the writers decided to off my husband Joe, in the final episode. I wasn't thrilled by this. Joe and I weren't given the heads up on how the last episode of Medium would unfold. Needless to say, I didn't think they'd kill off one of my family members. They couldn't kill one of the children's characters, that wouldn't sit right with people. They couldn't kill the heroine, Allison's the main character. They wouldn't kill the lady district attorney on the show since that was our show creator's real-life wife. I found out how the final episode ended through a friend on Facebook who worked on MEDIUM's set, a day or two before it aired. Although it's cool to have a show about my life and some very personal episodes centered around actual events in my life, it's hard to give up so much control. Clearly, some of the episodes stemmed from the creative minds of the writers. When a show is based on your life, the writers will exercise their creative license; best believe. I had to apologize to my brother Michael, a couple of times for episodes written about him (that I had no control over).

Was It Real?

People asked me every time an episode aired, was it real? Well, no, I don't get premonitions in my dreams; I have visions while I'm awake. I had more people at book signings, try to pawn off their sleeping pills on me. I politely declined. I sleep fine.

My husband, Joe, is a rocket scientist in real life. He's a brilliant man. He is a very doting father, Jake Weber portrayed Joe, surprisingly accurately. Joe is obviously patient, he's funny, he's so easy to like, and he's a tall drink of water. He doesn't "read" people. He can be around almost anybody. I can't imagine the freedom of not picking up on people's energy. I can get prickly around people because I absorb their energy, and I don't always like what I see or feel. It's not something that I can help, it's part of me. So, I stay around a very tight group of friends. I went to a friend's soiree once, and the women were, well, not warm (they reminded me of the generic trophy wives we see on TV). After an hour or so, I told my friend we were going to take off. Somehow, the women who ignored me and my bubbly friend, Amy, (for the last couple of hours), found out who I was. One of them (I don't know her name because I didn't stick around to find out), said "Oh, if, I'd known you were thee, Allison DuBois, I would've talked to you. You could've answered some questions for me."

Without a word, I pivoted on my heel and exited stage left! Buh-Bye.

Joe and I balance each other out, he's calm, cool and collected. I'm emotional, passionate, and I bring the heat! He backs, whatever, my play is, in life. He's always been entirely supportive of me and I, want him to do what makes him happy. At the moment, he's working on a spacecraft going to the moon! He's absolutely brilliant.

Our daughters inherited different facets of my abilities. Our youngest, Sophia, turned out to be the most empathic of the three girls. She will not follow in my footsteps professionally. Being an intuitive, it's just a part of who she is and how she sees the world.

Hurricane Allison, happening in our pilot episode and my being in Texas, working my first case with law enforcement, was real. Often, it's the parts of MEDIUM you're sure aren't real, that actually happened in my life. I found the first season resonated with me the most. I do, have an older brother Michael, who is an empath, he's funny, quite brave, and served in the military. He was a character who appeared, throughout the seasons, of the show. There really was a "Catherine" who is a medium, who first recognized my abilities. She was a good mentor for awhile. She wasn't thrilled when I surpassed her in the laboratory that was studying us and then me. Getting my own television show was the "straw that broke the camels back."

I hear she's doing well, I'm glad for her. I was surprised that the writers didn't include my parents in the storylines. Parents are sort of important in a person's life. My father's death impacted me profoundly. I had predicted that my dad would die of a massive heart attack at the age of 67. I spent two years trying to prevent his passing. I sent him to heart specialists, they said, "he's fine."

I lost my dad when I was 30 years old. He was 67.

My prediction turned out to be accurate; that's when I learned that some deaths are 'written in stone,' meaning they can't be prevented. My dad died when our youngest daughter Sophia was thre years old, she gave me messages from him. It was a beautiful, painful, time in my life, I wrote about my father's death in my first book, *Don't Kiss Them Good-Bye.*

I wrote a chapter for him titled "My Way."

I say beautiful because I was able to see my baby girl, talk to her granddad for the first time, passing his messages to me. After he died, Sophia perched herself on my knee and said, "Grandpa says, to stop crying inside."

My dad's death was a very transformative time in my life.

Many of the human storylines from the show, what I thought was the show's brilliance, was real. Such as my daughter Fallon aka Bridgette (played by the talented actress, Maria Lark) having an imaginary friend who turned out to be a dead child; that actually happened. There was an episode where she didn't want to take her bike helmet off. In reality, it was a pair of ladybug rain boots that she wore for days in a row. We had a hard time getting her to take them off to bathe. She was still, very young though, so it was kind of cute! Our girls having premonitions and seeing the dead was real. When my daughter Fallon was 3 years old, we were looking out our second-story bedroom window. She asked me, "Mommy, who is the man in our backyard?"

I smiled at Joe and looked down at our yard. I said to Joe, "It's an old man with denim overalls on."

Our housing development had been built on old farmland. No doubt, it used to be the deceased's pride and joy, and he was still tending to his crops. He didn't see the swing set he was walking through or the girls' toys, or Barbie Jeep scattered around him. He saw his land, just as it was, all those years ago. I explained this to Fallon, she ran looking for her big sister Aurora, screaming, "Aurora, there's a farmer in our yard!"

Aurora, our oldest, was two years old when she saw Joe's dad for the first time. It was night time, she started yelling for Joe. We opened her door, and she said, "There's a man in my closet."

Joe slowly opened the door. There was nobody there.

Aurora said, "He is wearing a bowtie and called himself, a jeen-e-us."

Joe took a step back and said, "My dad was known for wearing bowties and use to call himself a "Genius."

We were silent for a moment, and then I said to Aurora, "You saw grandpa Jim. He came to visit you."

She seemed both surprised and happy to know that she was special enough to warrant a visit! Joe was moved, that his dad and his daughter, had met after all.

It's just how our girls grew up, it was an accepted fact in our household, spirits were part of the world.

MEDIUM had struck a chord with people; it was the magic of our family, mixed with the allure of my abilities, that I think people found, relatable and captivating. A lot of people feel misunderstood, like a misfit, of some sort, so they could relate to my inability to fit into the world I was in. Our family changed lives, both our audiences and the people, who were hired to make the show a success. The people who worked on our show were some of the brightest talents in Hollywood. Great, salt of the earth people, with vision. Everyone who worked on the set, from lighting to make-up, producers, casting, actors, and every person on the set, made MEDIUM, one of a kind. They're very much like a family; they have MEDIUM reunions, every now and then. They laugh and catch up, talking about who's seen who and what they're up to.

Not being from an entertainment background, I didn't know what to expect on the set. It was interesting seeing the politics that goes on behind the scenes, Hollywood is a very nepotistic town.

MEDIUM also had some of the most gifted actors, who made special appearances throughout every season. MEDIUM "serial killer" Jason Priestly (90210), the iconic Molly Ringwald (Pretty in Pink), the incredibly talented Angelica Houston, Kurtwood Smith, Emma Stone, Jennifer Lawrence, and so many other phenomenal actors graced our show. The show was both riveting and touching, a rare combination.

A little known fact. I was played by two Academy award recipients, Patricia Arquette and Jennifer Lawrence (who portrayed Allison DuBois, as a teenager).

Today, my husband, Joe, is still a rocket scientist, and I continue to bring through the dead for clients and my event audiences. We're both living our passion through our careers. Our girls are grown now, our two youngest both graduated from college this year, early. We're very proud of our family. Growing up around Hollywood and on the set of MEDIUM became part of our children. Our youngest Sophia may not have been bitten by the Hollywood bug if it weren't for MEDIUM; now, she's headed to Los Angeles to pursue her film career. Putting her Communications and Film degree to use! Thankfully, her desire is behind the camera in a creative role. I don't need her following in my footsteps, dealing with stalkers and all the little extras that come with fame. As long as you're doing what you love, you'll always have a strong sense of purpose and contentment. But, since she's my child, I'm glad that her passion is behind, the camera. Although I have a sneaking suspicion, that somehow, she's going to be unable to avoid being in front of the camera too.

With Netflix, Hulu, and all of the ways, television shows are watched these days, there are new generations, connecting with the show MEDIUM. My hope is that young people with abilities will watch it, and realize, they're not alone and souls can be beautiful.

6

Are Your There?

COMMUNICATING ON YOUR OWN

*W*hat Does Grief Look Like? Well, let me tell you. The world holds no color, only shades of grey, a perpetual overcast day. An occasional happy moment brings back color temporarily. Then, when it's quiet, you remember why you were sad and then immediately everything is grey again. The clouds once again cover your eyes, bringing you back to your grief. This is why youth is so romantic. As time passes, you experience more heartache, leaving you pining for past days, which only held excitement and an eagerness to live! This is something that young people tend to have a bit of a monopoly on. Some of us who hold more of a "vintage" title, have fewer of those days because we carry a great deal of responsibility and bruises from life's lessons.

Time can make us more jaded, but also wiser. Grieving is akin to living in a world without music or being blessed with an innate talent. Then one day, never being able to do it again. You'd remember the music you loved or how your spirit would soar when you'd exercise your talent for others, but now, it's gone. Now, you have no choice but to just live with it. That's what we're told by the universe when we lose someone and have to live with their loss; we have no choice. The tears cried at your loved one's funerals have already been spent. I can't remove the pain people feel when they lose someone who holds their hearts. But, I can show you how you can be more accessible to the souls you seek to reconnect with. I'm often asked how people can connect to loved ones who've passed away? First, silence is golden, you have to be in a quiet space. Somewhere, you can really hear your thoughts and your inner voice. When the dead communicates, one way they convey messages is by making thoughts pop in your mind. It won't be anything that a chain of thoughts leads you to, it's out of the blue! The thought will carry the energy of someone familiar to you or pertain to someone you lost, so you know that it's them. Sometimes, one of these thoughts that I speak of will make you think, "Mom, would like that!" or "That sounds like something that Dad would say!"

Other times the thought takes you right back to a memory from your past. You'll feel like you were actually back in that moment. It feels so real because a deceased loved one is touching you, and you're both reliving the moment together. The deceased loved one is making the memory run through your mind. By connecting with you, they're making you feel as if they are right beside you, which they actually are; but you might think it was just a powerful flash from the past. It's a very emotional experience!

It's much harder for the deceased to communicate during the day because most people are distracted by traffic, kids, work, pets, the mayhem of living! This is why many people experience visits while in a dream state or when the house is eerily quiet. People who liked road trips when they were alive tend to ride passenger in your car. They tell me they like to "hear your thoughts and play songs for you."

While you're driving, you can actually hear their voice inside your mind or in your heart. The deceased just want to go, where you go, and still, be a part of your life.

If you want to communicate with a deceased loved one, it helps to gaze at a picture of them where they look full of life. This removes some of the barriers created by our grief that makes it hard for them to access us. Especially if you're still scarred by a traumatic image of them dying or seeing them, newly deceased. The reason the dead give me the age they reverted to after they died (Their version of heaven on earth) is so I can convey it to my client, then the client can take out a picture of their loved one at that age. I need to help the grieving to get to a place where they can dispense of traumatic images in their mind (from around their loved one's death). And instead get them to think of vivacious, happier snapshots of the deceased. Only then can we start breaking down the emotional wall around my client. It's not that the dead aren't around us. The problem is that people with raw pain and severe emotional trauma, (especially people with pain hiding behind a wall of anger), unintentionally block the dead from communicating with them. This is why the dead try and get messages through to their loved ones, by any means necessary.

Usually, through a friend of the family, a child connected to the family, a medium, anyone who will listen in an attempt to reach their hurting loved one. They'll even go through a barking dog in the family that barks and looks at you like, "Don't you see him?" Or, a freaked out cat that's always seemingly caught off guard, by an invisible force or is rubbing up against something lovingly, someone you can't see. I've even seen the deceased try to communicate with their family through a parrot or by sending loved ones text messages. Sometimes, a song will download itself onto your playlist. The deceased are very creative in finding ways to reach you.

You become more accessible to the dead when you smile thinking of them, more often, than cry. When you look at family photos of the best times of your life and laugh to yourself, thinking about how much crazy fun you all had together, this lowers your wall of pain. Usually, just enough for them to start communicating with you. Another emotional block comes from the living beating themselves up for not being able to save the one they love or feeling guilty for a fight they had around the time of the passing. I brought a dad through recently who spoke of his other son having a heavy heart filled with sorrow. I asked his brother why this was? It turned out his dad and brother had a disagreement before his dad died. His dad said, "That's what families do, they fight and they make-up!"

There's no grudge or residual anger felt by the deceased, only an all-encompassing love and a desire to remain part of their living loved one's lives. The sooner you let the guilt go, the sooner you'll have a visit from a loved one in the ethereal.

My Advice on being a Mom and an Intuitive

Many women have come to me for readings to try and under-stand their own gifts. I've noticed that I've evolved as a mother over the 20 years that I've been a professional medium. When I started doing readings, our girls were just babies! Now they're all grown up! So, I know a thing or two about raising kids and some of the challenges that mothers face. But, also, the guilt that mom's who work, experience every day. Being intuitive has real-ly been a great help when it comes to my family. Please, don't feel left out if you don't have abilities. Even with me being a fa-mous medium, my girls often rolled their eyes and ignored my advice. So, I received no special treatment from my kids. There was no pay off in the "I told you so" moments because they still got hurt, but sometimes, kids have to learn the hard way. That's just life! So, being a parent and an intuitive is just... being a par-ent.

How has being a clairvoyant mother been different from a mother without "abilities"? I don't think so different at all. Mom's are all designed with a bit of a sixth sense when it comes to their children. Most moms can feel when their child is in danger. There's a stirring in their soul, a knot in the pit of their stomach. A foreboding sense of dread that washes over parents as panic begins to swell inside of them. Being a parent is the universal equalizer for us as human beings. Even some species of animals will protect their children, or die trying. It doesn't matter where in the world you're from, how much money you have or who you know, the need to protect children is instinctual and affects us all. There, a word even skeptics can embrace, "instinctual."

I remember when our youngest daughter Sophia, was just learning how to walk. I was in the kitchen, making dinner. Her big sisters were watching Sesame Street videos, we were all waiting for Joe to come home. Just another typical day in suburbia. Sophia had been sitting with her sisters the last time I looked up from a boiling pot. I was on the phone with someone, I don't remember who. A feeling of fear gripped me, and in my mind, I saw Sophia standing in front of our house with the door open. I dropped the phone and bolted to the front door. I saw Sophia standing in our front yard almost to the sidewalk. She turned and smiled at me over her tiny shoulder. I scooped her up in my arms and just rocked her, reassuring myself that she was okay. That's the day we found out that Sophia knew how to unlock the deadbolt on our door! I think she felt Daddy coming and was trying to find him out front. Just then, Joe pulled into our driveway, with a grin on his face, and said, "What's going on? Are you out here waiting for me to come home?" Well, she was! So, yeah, that's what we're doing. I told him later what had happened. He chalked it up to a mother's intuition. You know what? That's really what it was. Our babies are part of us, not just when we're pregnant or hold them for the first time, but forever.

I say this to all moms with small children, "Stop, trying to be perfect!". A room littered with toys just needs a big plastic bucket in the corner to throw them in at the end of the day. No one will remember your messy house as long as it's clean (no food caked on the walls). In the future, your friends will be too busy on social media, trying to show you how perfect their kids are! They won't remember, toys and sippy cups littering your family room floor 15 years ago. So, like my daughter, Sophia, says,

"*CHILL* mom." Just enjoy the ride of motherhood, those little moments of playing with your kids are the magic that we take with us in our hearts when we take our last breath. It's the flaws in life that make your story interesting, colorful, and uniquely yours.

Being a working mom and a stay at home mom have different effects on us, I did both. I stayed home until our youngest daughter Sophia started Kindergarten, so roughly ten years. Then, I wrote my first book, *Don't Kiss Them Good-Bye*, my television show Medium aired, and I had to go on media tours and book tours around the world, that stretched out for weeks at a time. The guilt that I felt on the road, missing Joe and the kids, was sometimes unbearable. Joe took them to dance practice, did their homework with them, and took them to school in the morning. I was the collector of souvenirs, I brought Sophia home a rubber ducky, from every city I went to. You could fill her bathtub up with all the little ducks she had, twice!

My three daughter's t-shirt collections from all of my destinations overflowed. One day, I toured so much that there were no souvenirs from the hotel gift shops left to buy them that they didn't already have. They no longer greeted me at the door when I returned from touring. By the time our youngest daughter was in high school, I was getting burnt out on traveling. It was time to cool my jets and decide what I wanted to do with my life. That was easy, I wanted to spend more time with my family, and I really wanted to be a regular person. The everyday person part, never really worked out, but my life was more normal than it had been in a long time. I feel for working moms. Moms have a magnetic draw to their kids; we just do. What I can say to the new generations of moms is to make the time you spend with your kids memorable. Tell them you love them every day, be there when it counts and forgive yourself all of the times you can't be there.

When Sophia was a teenager, I was talking to her about touring, and I got a little teary-eyed. I remembered a time when I came home very late at night from my Australian tour. I tiptoed into her room to give her a kiss. I didn't want to wake her. She was holding a framed 8x10 picture of me while she slept. I had to wake her up and hug her. I didn't want her to sleep one more night missing me, thinking I wasn't home. Sophia looked at me in our conversation and said, "Mom, I don't remember you not being there. You were always there. You checked us out of school for our 'dental appointment' and took us to the fair. You did my hair for dance recitals. You cooked dinner. I don't really remember you not being there."

All of those years, all of my guilt, and she didn't even remember. So, moms, go on that girl's retreat! Take a vacation with your husband while you can still rock that bikini. Don't think that two-year old's tears won't dry. Just make the good times great, and be there when it counts.

Children breathe life into what can be an overly serious world. They remind us of who we use to be, when all animals and earthly wonders, were awe-inspiring. They overflow with energy and with thinking that all things are possible. If you don't have children of your own and you're looking for some zest in your life, I highly recommend joining a Boys and Girls Club to mentor children. What you give to them you get back ten fold through their appreciation. It's amazing just watching them grow and learn. We're here to learn and teach, it's our natural instinct. Maybe someone you mentor will be one of your little soulmates just waiting to be found.

Write a note to someone you love.

_____

_____

_____

_____

_____

_____

7

I'm Dying

I've read many terminal people and let me tell you, it's a very humbling experience. They're afraid, and they don't know what to expect. If I've read someone who's dying, it's obviously a slow, drawn-out death. Some people say they'd prefer it, so they can get their affairs in order and say good-bye to those they love. But, when you talk to someone terminal, you must wonder if you'd really want to die a slow death. The cost is high, depending on the level of pain that you must go through to have closure. I read a sweet man, I'll call him "Clark."

Clark's disease (ALS) was slowly paralyzing his ability to swallow and move. He was alone in his apartment with his pet rabbits. As I read him, I couldn't help but empathize with him. I wished that I had a Bat Antidote to share with him or I could tell him that he was going to get better. I read people who have cancer that I hear back from, who went into remission. I'm always so glad for them that they have more time or were granted some sort of reprieve, to fully enjoy life. They're the lucky survivors. This was different; there were no words that I could say to give him any hope. I could only tell him what would happen after he died. I attempted to describe to him what the glimpses of color on the Otherside look like. I had only ever shared this in-depth with my husband, Joe. I tried to describe to Clark what color looks like on the Otherside. I told him that colors 'pop' more on the Otherside.

When you look at red, it feels like a cinnamon breeze and makes you feel loved. Pink, make you feel a wave of playing on the playground as a child running with your friends, with the melody of children's laughter. Orange feels alive, and you feel like you just drank a fresh orange freeze, waking up every taste bud in your mouth. Looking at Yellow, makes you feel as though a friendly sun reached down and kissed you on the cheek, it calms you. Green, smells of pine trees, reminds you of camping and makes you feel adventurous. Blue on the Otherside is like no blue your eyes have seen before. No ocean can match it, no sky has come close. Blue makes your heart soar as though anything is possible and cools your mind. It fills you with all-consuming contentment. Purple feels enchanting. It makes you remember everything that you hoped for throughout your life. Purple is all of your birthday wishes, your conversations with God, your wishes on shooting stars, tossing pennies in a fountain, collectively coming together. It's the color of infinite faith. Each color emits a memory when you see it, they all have a purpose. They're triggers of our emotions and life experiences. Each color seems to represent a feeling. I don't know if the colors are seen the same by all mediums, I only have my perspective.

I told him all of the places that he had happy memories of, from childhood on up, would be there waiting for him, to experience again. Precisely as it was when he created the memory. I explained that his body would look and feel as it did when he was the most vibrant, whether that be 35 or 9. It was up to him! All of the people and animals that mortality took from him will be returned. It seemed to comfort him to know that he'd be restored in death. That death isn't the end, it's just the beginning of a new existence. I told Clark that he'd be able to still see the living people he loves; whenever he desires. Spirits have no limitations from time or physical barriers. They can be where they want when they want. If a Christmas party in 1962 was a perfect night to them, they could relive it, and everything will be exactly as it was on that night. If their wedding day in 1984 was blissfully happy and "heaven on earth," for them, then they can take a walk down the aisle again.

"Heaven" is a collection of the most meaningful moments of your life. Even something as small as making a tent with your brother, and sleeping under the stars, in your parents' backyard can be a piece of heaven. All our happy moments in life belong to us. In all of the readings that I do, the people I bring through show me glimpses from their past. It's a unique experience to be a voyeur and witness versions of someone's heaven. Knowing that Clark would soon die, gave me mixed emotions. I was sad that his living story was going to end in such a painful way. I was relieved to know that it would only take seconds after his death for him to be restored to a vibrant being. Seconds, until he sees all of the people who preceded him in death, who will step forward to embrace him. Seconds, for him to be filled with joy and an acute awareness that his pain was over.

After I brought through some relatives for Clark, who were

waiting for him and we talked about what happens after we die, I hesitated to hang up the phone. I knew I made him feel better, but I also was aware that I'd never talk to him again. Not many living people would. I told him that I'd pray for grace for him and a gentle transition. I also let him know that I would never forget him.

There are many people like Clark out there, who are afraid, who are dying. You may not be able to remove their disease or heal them, but you can show them kindness. If you can help a dying person to have an easier transition, consider it a gift to both of you.

We get so used to living, that the thought of letting go, feels unnatural for many. The fear of growing old seems universal, but what we don't always consider is that growing old is a luxury. It affords us more time with the people we love. Growing old allows us to travel, to feel sunshine on our face, to inhale the cold rising from the snow, to hear children laugh, to touch someone's life. There are so many beautiful experiences that sometimes youth takes for granted. When we're young, we concentrate more on what we look like or how we're seen by others. As we get older, we're supposed to attain wisdom, become more profound, more introspective of our worth. So, although aging can diminish our outer beauty, it increases our inner light. No matter how old you get, as long as you radiate your light to others, your beauty stays intact. When we die, that light that we worked so hard to share and understand, is what survives. As long as you're alive, your soul is a work in progress. So, every day, find a way to shine!

I ache for people who are dying, my only comfort is that I

know what's waiting for them. The dead will often tell me that "Dying wasn't so bad, it was like going to sleep and waking up renewed." They went to sleep in an old or sick body and woke-up vibrant and younger! The only pain we have after we die is either tethered to regret from how we lived or the suffering we see our loved ones go through, mourning our death. That's why the deceased work so hard to let us know that they're fine.

I have some advice, not just for the terminal but for all of us. Leave the living pieces of yourself in places that your loved ones can find them when they need it. I wrote on the back of 8x10 photographs that are in frames. I know, one day, when I'm gone, my girls or Joe, will see what I wrote on the back of those pictures. I'm acutely aware that the dead can draw our attention to objects such as pictures when they think we need a message or 'sign' from them. So, I'm leaving behind ways for me to communicate with them. Maybe, I'll knock one off the wall, just to state my presence, with flair!

If I was terminal, I would make video messages to be given to our daughters, for special milestones in their lives. Advice, for them, words of comfort and love, to elevate them when they need it. Words of praise, for their accomplishments and reassurance that I'm there, seeing it all.

I've already made books, with my recipes and pictures of what the dish should look like, when it's done, just in case they forget. I printed mine on Shutterfly, easy peasy! The dead talk about food a lot, and I hear the living say "they wished they had written down, Mom or Grandma's recipes." There's emotion in family recipes, so make sure you preserve them and duplicate them for each child.

I've labeled sentimental family jewelry, so our kids know who it belonged to and the story behind the jewelry, their dad gave me, through the years. I also told them to keep it in the family! Let your kids know what you want and who you want to have specific items. If there's jewelry you don't wear, and you know who you want to give it to, if they're responsible, give it to them now. That way, you get to watch them enjoy it. When someone dies, sometimes family does the wrong thing and takes something they weren't entitled to have. This can cause a permanent rift in the family. Avoiding future pain and division in the family is always a good thing. I'm also a firm believer that executors of estates should never be the children. Some people see it as picking a favorite child, and that in itself hurts feelings. An executor who's a trusted family lawyer or best-friend of the deceased removes the family, in-fighting. Family jewelry is another topic the dead often bring up because their jewelry carries their energy. They talk about who they wanted to have what, who didn't receive what they should have etc. The living is susceptible to emotional scars when they don't get a piece of jewelry that made them feel close to their loved ones. So, make a preempted strike to avoid the hurt feelings in advance.

DYING TO STAY

I found the first reading that I did, specifically, to help someone terminal to get comfortable with dying, the hardest. Not because terminal people are harder to read, but because I was forming an emotional attachment to someone who was going to die soon. I actually care about my clients, as each one teaches me something about life, and I share in their sentimental family memories for a moment. You forge a bit of a bond through such an intimate process.

I'm used to helping the living heal and re-engage in life after losing someone they love, that's hard enough; feeling their pain and grief. Try looking into the eyes of someone afraid to die, a person who can't be saved by any means. They search my eyes for answers, and I do my best to give them the answers they need.

My cousin Mark (who use to take care of my booking) called and told me that he wanted to book a reading for a man, who had very little time to live. The idea of doing a reading for a terminally ill person, honestly, scared me. It felt like a lot to carry. All I could think was, "What if I said the wrong thing to him? What if he got angry at death and took it out on me? What if he broke down and cried, how could I console, this man?" There are so many emotions wrapped up in death, and I didn't want to, in any way, hurt, this man, who was in a delicate stage of life.

I initially said no.

I said no, because I'm familiar with bringing through the dead, but I was being asked to counsel the dying. Many aspects of this request petrified me. What if Jim didn't like me? Or if he couldn't get past his scientific background and embrace faith instead? What if I said something that made it worse for him? The dying wasn't my forte; it was unfamiliar ground for me. The what if's? Kept piling up, my nerves were getting the best of me.

On top of those fears, the man's name was 'Jim,' and he had pancreatic cancer, just like my father in law, the one I never met in life, had died from. Could I handle it? I had missed meeting Joe's dad by only three months. In my heart, I've always known that Joe's dad wouldn't have wanted to meet me in his dire condition. I also have a sneaking suspicion that Jim brought Joe and me together. Our daughter, Fallon, was born five years to the day after my father in law, Jim, had died. In the same hospital, he died. Coincidence? I don't think so.

Part of me wasn't sure that this wouldn't affect Joe, seeing a man of similar age, name, and illness pass through our home and our lives. Or maybe, it could help Joe process his father's passing, something he had never entirely been able to do. He missed his dad so much. I spent weeks thinking about this, weighing the pros and cons.

Fortunately, my cousin, Mark, is quite persuasive. He's able to talk most people into just about anything with his charisma, and that's precisely what he did with me. Despite all of my reservations, I agreed to read Jim and set aside my uncertainties. After all, he was dealing with a time issue here, so now was not the time to make it about me.

Jim came to my house, on September 10th, two weeks before the anniversary of my own dad's passing. I had raw emotions. I was still grieving for my own dad, but my nervousness and concern for Jim got top billing.

I noticed that Jim had the kindest blue eyes. He's one of those people you look at and KNOW he's a doctor. Jim exuded an air of academia, an "I don't have time to waste" vibe. He sat down across from me, and we talked for a few minutes. I wanted to put him at ease, that this 'process' was not going to be 'weird.' This was his first reading and, likely, his only reading. We discussed what happens when a person dies? How can the dead, reconnect with the living? How, souls, can still participate in the lives of their loved ones? Jim knowing that he would always be able to be around his family, seemed to calm his nerves a little. As the reading progressed, he seemed more and more at ease. He even seemed amused by the information from his deceased family members in the reading.

I razzed him, "See, it doesn't hurt a bit! This is a completely painless process." We both laughed.

I brought through a few of his relatives. I described their personalities, gave him names and other details. The more I conveyed to him, the less stressed, he looked. His face, once wrenched with worry, now, had relaxed. Jim's reading was personally a precious experience, one that has changed me for the better.

I was afraid to face Jim's fear, feel his pain, and be helpless not to be able to save him. But then, I realized his life wasn't completely slipping away; it was simply changing forms. He'd still exist in our world. I felt honored that with Jim's limited time, he spent part of it with me, talking about life and death. Talking about his wife and kids. How much, he loves all of them, savors every conversation with them, every moment. When we were finished with the reading, I hugged Jim good-bye. I wanted to hold on to him and keep him here, but terminal illness doesn't work that way.

I saw Jim six weeks later. He looked different. He had lost some of the color in his face, but he still looked happy. He was still among the living. We went to a fundraiser, for what else? Pancreatic cancer research. We had a lovely yet emotionally draining evening. He and his wife Dot stopped by the next day to drop off souvenirs for our family (from their favorite football team), the Texas Longhorns—such a sweet gesture.

January rolled around. It's my favorite month because I was born in it!

January 22nd was a Saturday, and it was on the night of my birthday party, that Jim let go. I remembered, back to when I met Dot. I kept seeing the number '2' connected to Jim. Then, I found out that they were married on the 22nd of March. My dad had passed on the 22nd of September. Now, Jim, on the 22nd of January. Jim had delivered babies for decades, witnessing life coming into the world. How exhilarating! It made sense, why death, life exiting the world, didn't feel right to him; because it's not what he knew.

Days after Jim passed away, Dot told me that Jim had shared with her that meeting with me took away a lot of his fear of dying. To hear those words, was just one more life moment, that made my life, profoundly worth living. It's nice to know that each of us can touch another's life for the better. We're all called on to help someone, at some time, in our lives. Everyone's looking for their "path." But, you can only find it when you engage with other people. Strangers can help us to see, what we're made of, what our strengths and weaknesses are; they can help us figure out what we want out of life! The only person who keeps us from achieving our goals is ourselves when we stand in our own way. Get out of your way, and shine. Be who you are and if it's not good enough for some people, who cares? If I hadn't read Jim, because I was afraid, I would've never known that special, warmhearted man. He and I had a moment of clarity and understanding together, facing his mortality. He lived an incredible life, he was grateful for every moment. Life isn't just an existence, at least, it's not supposed to be. Life should be full of emotions and connections with others. We can learn lessons, from the good and the bad in our lives. All of it makes each of our lives unique.

"Jim, thank you for the memories, the life lessons, and for pushing me to be better, in every aspect of my life."

I thought it was essential to include a chapter on dying. Terminal people are given a life expectation time frame by their doctor. To those who are dying, they might as well be wearing a clock on their chest, telling the world they're going to expire, as it counts down to their last minute of life. They're afraid, they're worried about the people they love. They wonder how their family will get along without them. What moments will they miss by not being there? Graduations? Weddings? Babies being born? Some people who aren't rich with friends and family might think about how they lived their lives, who they loved, and what regrets they might have. That's the thing about life, the choices we make we sometimes regret.

Time only moves forward, not backward, you can't have a redo. So many things in life can be fixed. You can't go back in time and marry the person you let slip through your fingers all those years ago. Have the family together you wished you had. You can't go back and be there for the children you abandoned. You can call them and apologize now, but you can't undo the past. When you're dying, you wonder how the time you have left will be best spent. Dying can be scary. Your family and friends can be with you, but it's something that you have to do alone, kind of like being born. It's an experience that's beyond our control. I wrote this chapter because the dying matter. I wanted to highlight them, recognizing that they're not invisible. They don't have to suffer alone in silence. Churches have clergy for them to talk to, parks are full of strangers wanting to listen, many good people care. When I looked up resources, I was touched to see so many DYING support groups listed. If you know someone terminal, please direct them to the many online resources. Get them hooked up with the technology, care for their soul, and ease their mind. Let them know that they're not alone.

A MEDIUM AND A BEAUTY QUEEN WALK INTO A BAR...

Life can be very sobering when facing our mortality. When we're young, we often hear older people say, "Time goes by fast; make sure you enjoy it!"

At 20 years old, you think, "How can 20-40 years just fly by?" and we laugh. Well, they're not kidding.

When I was 13 years old, I met a girl named Debbie Fallon in the 7th grade. We were friendly to one another but not close. Fast forward to our 20th high school reunion. I reconnected with a couple of childhood friends, we had all come so far in life. We were all three moms! One of those people was Debbie. Little did I know, but the fresh-faced beauty queen that I remembered from high school, had been through a lot of personal losses. I offered her a job working for me as an assistant, and our friendship grew as we spent time together. We would share many emotional conversations over cocktails, comparing notes of what we went through in high school and since then. A few years later she gave birth to twin sons, she loved being a mom. She adored her four boys, they were the lights of her life.

A couple of years later, she was diagnosed with lung cancer. She asked me to come to the hospital to sit with her, she was going in for surgery to save her life. They only let family in so, on that day, I was her "sister." We looked nothing alike, we laughed about getting away with our fib. It was the same laugh two sixteen-year-old girls in high school would have after successfully sneaking out. I just wanted to be there for my friend.

Debbie braved chemo and surgery for years, to try and be here longer for her boys. Cancer had moved to her brain, she had a tumor. We had many in-depth talks about life after death. She saw me conduct readings over the years bringing through the dead when she worked for me. She was familiar with what happens after we die. Still, she wanted to be here with her sons. She was comforted though knowing that if she lost her battle with cancer, her dad and brother would be waiting for her.

Move forward to June 2019. I threw my husband Joe a birthday party, complete with mylar airplane balloons, happy hour with friends and family at Scottsdale Airpark, a Gemini's dream! Debbie was also a Gemini, so I brought her roses. This would be the last picture that I would take with Debbie.

In September, Debbie wanted to go on a double date for dinner at Durant's. I made a reservation. When I found Debbie waiting at the bar, even though she had brain surgery at the end of June, she looked like a beautiful rockstar. Her head was partially shaved from surgery, but somehow, she made it look like an intended style. I told her that she looked like a rockstar, she laughed. I was sharing the last date, she would ever go on. October rolled around, Joe was out of town on business. Debbie came and stayed with me for a couple of days since I live close to her clinic for chemotherapy. I made her the macaroni salad she likes for dinner. We talked about her boys, failed relationships, and I tried to stay positive for her that she would have more time. She was worried about her boys, how they'd be if she died. I told her that if something happened to her, I'd ask everyone to bring Debbie's pictures from throughout her life and give them to her sons to help them grieve. I hoped this would enable her sons to move through their grief, knowing how much their mother was loved. This idea seemed to calm her. I prayed hard; she'd be gifted more time. We curled up on the couch and watched The Marvelous Mrs. Maisel and Stranger Things Two. The final episode (it was set close to the same year we had our Jr. high dances, the music, and the hair), it was a blast from the past. I savored my time with her.

She sent me a text at the end of January, wanting to get together. I was on my way out of town for my birthday trip to Sedona. After that I couldn't see her because we had been hit by a pandemic and she was vulnerable, so we couldn't risk it.

April 9, 2019, I reached out to Debbie to inform her that one of her friends from high school had passed away. Debbie told me she had started to lose her eyesight. Even though I deal with death regularly, I wouldn't let my mind think anything other than, "the doctors will fix it, she'll be fine." I knew better than that.

April 29th, (ironically my daughter Fallon's birthday) would be our last conversation. Debbie knew I didn't name my daughter Fallon after her (Fallon is Debbie's maiden name), she still would say, "of course you did!" It was a running joke between us.

May 14th, I was getting ready to go into my recording studio to record the chapter DYING for my new audiobook (Love Can't Tell Time). I got a call from Debbie's ex, he said she was in the hospital. He told me she wasn't going to regain consciousness. She had no brain activity. To say I was destroyed doesn't even come close to describing the painful scream of grief that began to engulf me from within.

May 15th, my eyes were swollen from crying the night before. I took a deep breath, got dressed, and entered the studio to record DYING and dedicate it to Debbie. When I started writing my sixth book a year ago, I had no idea that Debbie would be in it. I wouldn't let myself see it, I didn't want to hear it, my heart wouldn't believe it. Here I was, memorializing my childhood friend in a chapter that I had written six months before. I was talking about past terminal clients of mine that I helped prepare for death. I wrote the chapter so that terminal people might feel comforted knowing that they wouldn't disappear when they die; they would, in fact, thrive.

After I finished recording the chapter, I walked out of my office with a tear-stained face. I texted Debbie's ex to inquire about how Debbie was doing. I needed to hear from someone who was with her or close to her at that moment. He told me, "Debbie, was gone." Debbie was crossing over while I was in the recording studio. My friend was letting go of life while I was dedicating the DYING chapter to her. As I was telling her how much we all loved her and to "visit us often." Strangely, this made sense, two friends in a fragile moment, acknowledging to one another that things between us had changed.

A week later, I saw Debbie, she looked younger. I imagine it was the age she was when she got married all those years ago and started having children. She smiled at me and stepped to the side, revealing her dad behind her. She was telling me that he came to greet her when she crossed. She showed me her dad wrapping his arms around her and hugging her. Then, her brother walked into frame and smiled at me, as if to say, "She'll be alright, we've got her."

That night Debbie told me to play the song "Hold Me Now" by the Thompson Twins. A tune that would've been popular when we were in junior high. I told Alexa to play it. I listened intently to the lyrics. I was floored that it seemed tailored to us as friends. The laughter, the pictures we took together, us both looking for a "perfect world we'd never find" and her having to leave. It was hauntingly beautiful.

I shared this personal experience with you to show you how mediums grieve. We grieve and feel pain just as everybody else does. We can see them, we can hear them, it helps knowing where they're at and what they're doing, but we're not immune to the pain that accompanies loss.

Debbie never wallowed in self-pity, she had grace and dignity, during an impossible fight to live. She was a bright light, funny, smart, sarcastic, her beauty goes without saying. She was a pageant queen, but she was so much more than that. Debbie was irreverent but always a lady. People facing a terminal illness have to fight their battle alone; they go to sleep with what's going to kill them, and they wake up with it still inside of them. It helps them to know that they matter to many and they won't be forgotten. If you know someone terminal, don't think that they will have another year. Show them now what they mean to you. I did, Debbie knew I cared. I showed her, through visits, sleepovers, bringing over groceries, meals, and I even sent a cleaning crew over so she would have one less thing to do. I feel at peace, knowing that Debbie died knowing that she was family to me. If you're faced with a similar situation, stop your busy life and take the time to let them know now how much you cherish them. You'll never regret it.

What does love mean to you?

_____

_____

_____

_____

_____

_____

8

Coping With Death

Grief, in a nutshell:
"The only walls built between the Otherside and us,
are constructed by the living."

– Allison DuBois

THE SIX STAGES OF GRIEF

*M*any bereavement counselors believe there are five stages of grief, but I think there are six. My six stages of grieving are—denial, anger, bargaining, depression, acceptance, and reconnection. Reconnection is the stage that most counselors don't include, but for me, and for those I bring through, it's the catalyst needed to work through the grief of losing a loved one. I feel it's the most crucial because it re-establishes the relationship and answers questions that the living has around their deceased loved one.

DENIAL

I experienced this myself when my dad, Mike, passed away. He died suddenly, so there was no preparing to lose him. Even though I had predicted two years before that he would die at 67 of a massive heart attack, I was not prepared to lose my dad. I had sent him to heart specialists, they said he was fine.

One morning I was slapped in the face by a phone call telling me that my dad had died. My response was, "You mean my grandma died."

I sat on the plane to Phoenix and was mentally preparing myself to make Dad's funeral arrangements, I still thought, 'This has got to be a mistake, he's healthy, he's been a ballroom dancer for 50 years.'

I looked at my dad in his casket, I couldn't grasp that the person I was looking at was really him. My dad was so full of life, and the man that I saw wasn't laughing, or able to Cha Cha, as he walked.

My denial started to fade, but there were still mornings when I would wake up and think that it was all a bad dream. I would pick up the phone and dial my dad's number, hoping that he would answer; he didn't. Some people who are in denial will continue to live their lives. Some will make everything about the deceased and forget about their grieving family members. This can be painful for living family members, who feel invisible.

You know in your mind that your loved one is deceased, but your heart won't accept, not seeing them again. So a struggle between reality and wishful thinking ensues until you no longer have the energy to fuel your inner conflict. Once you're exhausted, reality sets in and stays like an unwelcome house guest. You place their things in front of you and hold their house keys, their comb, the last note in their wallet that they took out of the bank, right before they died. You pour over their daily items, probing them with your fingertips, trying to feel your loved one's energy.

THE DECEASED'S PERSPECTIVE

Think of the deceased as they helplessly watch us struggle with their loss. The dead have to walk with us through our stages of grieving. They're aware that we need them for strength. They lost their life. Now they feel responsible for our dying inside because of them. They see our denial, see us reach for them, and watch us pick up the phone to call them. The deceased aren't provided the luxury of denial. They're very aware of who's among the living and who exists in spirit. My father had to watch me fall apart, as I tried to convince myself that he wasn't really, gone. He probably wanted to be on the other end of my phone call to a ghost, so that he could answer me and make my anguish disappear. 'Denial' is a stage that fights to give us moments of peace as we begin a very long journey back to our deceased loved one.

ANGER

I was angry with God, as I sat in church I told God, that I wasn't going to talk to the dead anymore, I wasn't going to do the work that he wanted me to do because he took my dad. Why not take a pedophile? A murderer? Why did it always seem to be the good ones who paid the price? I was also angry with family members, who had previously stressed out my dad; maybe all of the years of stress caused his heart attack? I was mad at Joe for loving me. I didn't want to care about anyone who could leave me so completely destroyed if I lost them. When you hit your anger phase, nobody can reason with you, because your emotions are too raw. I used to scream, 'I want to rip the roof off heaven and bring him back!'.

For me, denial and anger were acting in concert. The effects were evident on the plane ride home, my dad had been dead for less than 24 hours. A woman wanted the window seat next to me, and though I was barely functioning, I bent my knees and pulled my feet up on my seat so she could get past me. She said, "I'd prefer that you stood up!"

I told her, "I'd prefer that my dad wasn't dead!"

She sat somewhere else.

When a person is going through the anger phase, they misplace their tact, this is very normal. If it happens to you, don't beat yourself up, it's a part of processing grief. Just try not to break any laws while processing. I found that anger was more than a phase. It was a reoccurring emotion that was peppered throughout the grieving process— until you're ready for stage six, reconnection.

THE DECEASED'S PERSPECTIVE

The anger phase is difficult for the deceased to watch. The departed knew you as an upbeat, loving person in their life, and now you're hard for them to recognize. They want you back the way you were before; before they died, before all of the pain. The deceased move through the stages of grief with you, it helps them process their physical death. So, in essence, you're going through it together, side by side. My father knows that I can be a willful person, so the 'Anger' phase must have made him cringe. I'm not very good at keeping my feelings bottled up inside of me. When you're going through the anger phase, you become a live wire, and you affect everyone around you.

I know that my dad understood my pain, but imagine having to watch your child be torn apart by your loss. The grieving can't be reached by the Otherside. When we go through the anger phase, the dead kick it into high gear to get messages to you, any way, they can. My dad stood beside me, as I watched women twice my age, laugh with their dads over lunch. You're not angry at others for having what you no longer do. You just can't understand why you had to be one of the living, left feeling robbed by death. I thought, "Why did my dad have to die? I'm only 30 years old. Two of my daughters won't even remember him. They'll never know how funny he is. He can never teach them how to dance like he taught me. My dad was in great physical shape. He's a ballroom dancer for God's sake!."

I was beyond angry, in a place where you question if anything is fair in this world? Many people go through a cycle in life where something terrible happens to them. Sometimes this makes everything look ugly around them. They begin to wonder if there's any fairness, any goodness, any justice, did anything matter? Did anyone good ever win? Everyone takes a turn losing someone they love, this time, it just happened to be my turn.

BARGAINING

I think most people try to bargain with God. I swore that if God brought my dad back, I would only do good. I would keep doing the "work" helping others, and we could forget about all the pain in my heart, the lump in my throat, and the knot in my stomach. I wouldn't even be mad at God, all would be fine. I just needed him to bring my dad back! Bargaining doesn't work, but you have to try; you'll try anything. Bargaining is a strange place to find yourself, your desperation to hold on to your loved one, overrules your mind, telling you that negotiation doesn't work.

THE DECEASED'S PERSPECTIVE

The bargaining phase makes the deceased shake their head, they know it doesn't work, and they know this is the one time that most people talk to God, to try to strike this unnatural bargain. For me, bargaining was the shortest phase. Once I made my demands clear to God, I knew that I was on my own. I quickly moved on to depression. Bargaining usually takes place right after our loved one dies. The grieving will try anything to bring their loved ones back. Bargaining is born out of desperation and love. My dad had to witness my painful plea to a higher power, as I tried to will him back to life. He would have felt helpless and sad, seeing me struggle, knowing that there was no other way for me to heal. Grieving is natural and necessary, but it's a long process, it's emotionally taxing. This phase comes and goes for years. Our deceased loved ones lend us their energy to give us a push forward. Even then, you're not sure if you'll have enough strength, to move on with the living.

DEPRESSION

Oh, the deep levels of sadness that you will feel! You feel dead inside, you walk around in a heart-wrenching fog, waiting for something to change inside of you. You take inventory of your memories, making sure that you remember everything about the person you've lost. Your depression makes you push away everyone who cares about you; you don't want to be loved anymore. The dark cloud of depression can consume you, you'll cry at the drop of a hat, or the mere mention of their name. You wonder why you're here at all? You feel guilty if you laugh, you quickly put yourself back in the corner of depression, for even thinking of feeling good.

Depression is a heavy phase to move through. It feels like your heart is walking on broken glass, you'll have the scars to prove that you didn't walk out of the loss, unscathed.

I've noticed that a lot of grieving people, in this phase, go to Disneyland, so I did the same thing with my family after my dad died. I know that might sound strange, but when all you feel is sorrow, you think that maybe 'The Happiest Place on Earth' can remind you of what life is about. Instead of sitting in your house and staring at the wall, you sit on a park bench and watch children play. It's healing to see, the pride spread across parents' faces as they take snapshots of their children, the little beings they love the most. Taking my family to Disneyland helped to pull me out of my paralyzing haze of sadness. As I sat, watching our three girls laughing, thriving, living, it reminded me, that's what I was, to my dad. I was that magic to him when he was alive, and I realized that I am still that to him now. The warmth that fills a parent's heart, that's us. Even when we're grown, we're still their kids. Give them something to smile about.

THE DECEASED'S PERSPECTIVE

It's tough for our deceased loved ones to witness our depression. They feel for us; they yearn to take our pain away. They hear our thoughts, and they see us stumble as we grapple with their loss. I use to sit in my car and listen to Karen Carpenter sing, Solitaire. I'd play it on repeat and cry missing my dad. He saw me. Throughout my depression, my dad was there. He saw me mentally checkout, he saw me push Joe away. He watched me smile, trying to enjoy Christmas three months after he died, even though I was crying on the inside. I've looked at pictures of me from that Christmas morning after he died. I looked withdrawn, colorless, emotionless. That was my invisible Christmas; to me, it never happened, no Christmas cheer. His birthday was Christmas Eve, I had a party at an old haunt of his. Sometimes alcohol helped to not feel, so I got through his birthday, alright surrounded by friends. My dad saw how much he was loved and what a big part of our lives he was. All he could do was watch me hurt. He'd try to get through to a daughter, who wouldn't be able to hear him for another few years; because her wall of grief was impenetrable.

ACCEPTANCE

Acceptance is a double-edged sword—you're able to move forward, but you feel like you're leaving them in the past. Acceptance can make you feel empty inside because you feel as though you've given up the battle to hold on to them. In reality, you're moving towards them.

When you get to the part of grieving, where you can accept your loved one's passing, I recommend that you immediately begin the reconnection process. Once you've wrapped your mind around your loved one's physical death, you can start to really interact with their spirit. Acceptance is necessary when it comes to communicating with them in a whole new way. Now, it's time to memorialize them with joy, and you will slowly start to hear and feel a soft voice speaking to you from within your heart. The more you talk to them about your day, the louder the voice becomes, and as it gets louder, you'll find that your heart begins to heal.

If you want to connect with your loved one, do what the deceased loved in life. Activities like listening to their favorite music, making their favorite dinner, anything they loved. You will start to feel their energy around you. Acceptance allows you to begin rebuilding your life with them spiritually. It will make them a big part of your daily life. We get to bring them with us on our journey. They can share in your laughter, your victories, and, yes, your defeats too. They can be there for you and buffer your setbacks. They have the power to lend us their energy when we need it. Just when we think we can't get through a hard time, they give us that extra little push!

THE DECEASED'S PERSPECTIVE

After the first year, acceptance is forced on you, you can no longer pretend that they're on a cruise or away on business. The second-year hits you hard, acceptance knocks the air out of you, literally. You'll find yourself taking shallow breaths. The deceased know the acceptance phase is painful for us; they also know that it's necessary. Without acceptance, they can't access us to communicate; the dead holds our hand through this phase. For me, it became easier to feel my dad around me once I was thrust into acceptance. Even after this phase, you will have your good and bad days. Some days, I was able to see the blessings around me; other days, everything was grey and felt without meaning. My dad watched me miss out on many days with my babies because I couldn't function. At about that time, *Medium aired for the first time*. It had been two years and three months since my dad died.

RECONNECTION

After acceptance, comes reconnection, you will begin to reach for the spirit of the deceased and start listening for them in your head and heart. Every fiber of your being is prepared to receive a 'visit,' you're open to signs from your loved ones. You begin to acknowledge both the spirits and their attempts to get your attention.

Once you have arrived at this phase, your healing truly accelerates, and you feel them with you so strongly. Your pain starts to morph into a peaceful knowing—knowing that they're still a part of you and your life. You will now look forward to the signs, and smile when you get them, as you whisper a 'thank you' to your loved one, for coming through for you. Their birthday is no longer such a sad day, but a day to celebrate their life and the good times you shared. You will have an understanding that they're not in some ethereal place, but beside you, talking to you, touching your hand, and loving you. The phase of reconnection puts you on the same energy page as the deceased, accelerating the healing. The dead don't want you to miss out on life, feeling like you died inside, too; that's not what they want. They want you to thrive and show them the world through your eyes. You now give them bragging rights, on the Otherside. The deceased points out to those around them, the connection between the two of you is intact, your bond is unbreakable by death. This has a positive effect elevating others, it sends a ripple of energy through the spirits around them. It encourages the spirits, to try harder for their own reconnections.

THE DECEASED'S PERSPECTIVE

Our deceased loved ones welcome reconnecting with us. Having followed us through the previous stages of grief, they are relieved when we are ready to talk to them again. Imagine the joy that both the grieving and the deceased feel, when the lines of communication are re-established. Finally, they can show themselves to us, talk to us, and we are now capable of recognizing the signs that they work so hard to send us. It's not that they hadn't sent signs before. The problem is that grieving people are often blocked by pain. We are rendered unable to recognize their signs through our tears. Reconnection, heals, and soothes us, eases us back into a comfortable place that feels like home, one with them, still in it.

My reconnection came about four years after my dad died. I had already received obvious signs and many messages through other people, including my three-year-old daughter. My day came when I was at the mall, something I often did with my dad growing up. I stopped to look in a store window; my dad's reflection was looking back at me. Reconnection had been established, he knew he'd made contact, with me then. He seemed so relaxed, so content, all I could do was stand there staring at him. Even though he was there and I was looking right at him, I wanted so badly to touch him, but being a medium, I knew this could only be accomplished from within now. I knew that sometimes when you reach out to touch them, they disappear. So, I stood there and took him in with my eyes. Just a few... moments... longer. I've since found peace as I move toward seeing my dad again. I can hear him talking to me, calling me 'Jellybean' like when I was small. I hear him, more than I see him, probably because instinctually, children get upset when they see their parents and want to run to them. So, my dad talks to me, more often than appearing to me, to minimize my pain. My dad is still in my life, it takes more than death, to sever our ties, to those that we love. Once you've established 'reconnection,' you'll find most days, you're fine. The sadness of missing making memories with them, that still lingers. I often think, of how fun my dad was, teaching me how to dance, at his dance studio. My dad blotting his pizza with a napkin to remove the grease from the top. He said, "It might buy me some time, you never know!"

So, since I was a little girl, I've blotted my pizza just like my dad. Now, so do his granddaughters. Dad was right, I'm sure it did, buy him some time.

HELPING KIDS COPE WITH LOSS

I've included this section to help children cope with loss and navigate the six stages of grief. They're in their formative years, they need guidance from adults or other children who understand their pain. When you lose someone at a young age, it changes who you become, you also have less control over how you can deal with your feelings. They can't go to a bar and order a martini to dull the pain, they don't have a credit card to pay for a therapist, they don't have a car to take them to a place that soothes them. They have to look to the adults in their lives to help them sort through their emotions. Adults who are responsible for teaching children how to move forward don't always have the know-how. If you have a tool to help minimize a young soul's pain, it might prove invaluable in helping to preserve the relationship the child had with the deceased. Fostering the relationship between the child and the dead helps to remove feelings of abandonment that children sometimes have around loss.

Children are often the 'unseen' wounded when someone dies, we need to help them navigate their pain. They need to be recognized by adults, as affected by the loss. Grown-ups need to remember to 'take a knee' when dealing with someone smaller than them, get down on their level. Kids need to see you on their own terms and level. Children are naturally resilient, but they don't always know how to help themselves. It's our job to guide them and provide them with a support system and the coping skills that they need. Kids need to be able to talk about who they miss, without adults getting upset that they brought up the subject. Even if it's painful for you to talk about someone you lost, do it for the children and for the person you grieve for. Otherwise, you're teaching a child to bottle up their feelings, saying to them that your feelings are more important than theirs. Children need an outlet for their feelings. A journal to write their feelings in can be helpful for kids old enough to write. For very young children, an easel of paper with colored pencils, crayons, paints, etc. can be very therapeutic in their healing. They can draw pictures of where they imagine their loved one is, in the sunshine, in their house, under a rainbow, wherever their heart sees them. Don't underestimate this outlet. It's instrumental in helping children to communicate their feelings and visualize where their loved one is at. We don't want a funeral to be a child's last mental image of their loved one; they need to know that the dead reside in a place of color and light. This will help to ease the child's heart and lift their spirit.

For kids who suffer loss, I find that it helps them to have a shirt from the one they miss, mainly because it carries their scent and energy. You can stuff it like a pillow and tie off the ends with string or a ribbon, whatever you fancy. Kids can hold it while they sleep, this should make them feel closer to those they love, and comfort them. This will help them to sleep more soundly. Often holding on to an object of the deceased at bedtime opens a spiritual door for a 'visit' to occur while sleeping. Be careful about washing shirts that smell like the person who's died. Make sure the child says it's okay before you wash it or get rid of what they see, as their last remnants of their parent, etc., that could be somewhat traumatic for them.

Let the child pick a picture that they love of the deceased to keep in their room. If a grandparent died, it's sometimes better to give them a young picture of their grandparent. Especially a picture of their grandparent around the same age, the child is. They need a visual image of the person they love, that's lively and carries the essence of who they miss. Not, one from late in life. Remember, when you were small and ALL old people kind of looked like the Crypt Keeper or like they were from another planet? They look so different, from tiny you. Kids need a picture that they can relate to, someone appearing closer to their age. It will still carry the essence of their grandparent and bring back warm memories. With technology the way it is today, you might print out a photo album for the child to keep. When we miss someone, and we need to connect with them, we stare at their pictures. It makes us feel like we're touching the heart of the person we miss. Just so you know, you actually are touching them, when you look at their pictures. When you recall someone you love or look at their pictures, it pulls them to you. Spirits are empaths, they can experience what you're feeling for them.

A musical instrument can be helpful for anyone who is trying to work through a problem that's troubling them. It helps to express themselves constructively, allowing the troubled individual to work out their stress through music.

I also find that for children who are really struggling emotionally, a pet of their choosing brings them a great deal of peace. It doesn't matter if you already have a pet; the new pet gives them something to hold to help them heal. Give them something to invest their emotions in, their time, and their love. Pets are a great form of therapy for anyone who feels shaken by life.

I sent my young nephew a ceramic angel shaped keepsake box when his mom died. I told him that if he wants to give his mom a message, he can write it down and put it in the delicate container. I assured him that his mom would see what he's feeling. It's not that one must, write the thought down for it to be heard; it just gives the living a physical connection to the deceased. Sometimes, tangible communication makes more sense to children. We need it, the departed do not, but they still appreciate the sentiment. This gesture is especially helpful for children, who lose someone; it gives them back some power, a bit of control in their young life. I also told my nephew that he could write down his life wishes and place them in his angelic keepsake box, letting his mother know what he was up to and his thoughts.

I wanted to reach to the Otherside and pull Deidre back, but who doesn't feel that way when a loved one dies? Losing someone we love can make us want to rip the roof off of Heaven and reclaim those we miss. It's, unfortunately, not how life and death works. We can, however, reach them in other creative ways that draw us closer in spirit. I know that children need to have their personal grief and pain recognized by others. They also need to have a physical connection to their lost loved ones. Whether you make the child a pillow to sleep with or give them a beautiful picture frame with a picture of their deceased loved one in it, remember to do something. It really is a lifeline for them. The more stories that you can share with children about the people they miss, the more quickly they'll heal. This will bring them closer to the deceased, and it will actually make them feel quite close to you. When you connect a child to the departed through stories, they bond with you. You become a surrogate for them, their personal connection, to the person who died. You're also the person who loved them through their pain and grief. Something they will remember for the rest of their life long after you're gone.

I included these sections on coping with loss because no one is taught how to navigate grief. Whether you lost a soulmate or someone influential in your life, you still need to know what to do with your pain. You also need a guide to help you to reconnect with them in spirit. So, I thought it might be helpful if I acted as your guide. Think of my coping tips as a road map back to the one, you're not quite ready to let go of yet. The six stages of grieving apply to any age. People seem caught off guard when children display the same reaction to bargaining, anger, and depression as adults do. If children are taught to cope with grief, they grow to be adults who have the tools to adjust to the loss.

Grieving the loss of a loved one or even a pet that you cherished can be intense. When you're feeling so defeated and alone, it's helpful to know what a typical reaction is and what stage of grief you might expect next. This book is a book about souls. How to nurture them, how to connect with them, and how to heal them.

Write a note to someone you love.

_____

_____

_____

_____

_____

_____

_____

9

A Sight for Sore Eyes

WHAT TO EXPECT WHEN YOU SEE YOUR LOVED ONE AGAIN, BOTH IN DREAMS AND AFTER DEATH

Since this is a book about soulmates, I thought it pivotal for my readers to know what you might expect when you see the spirit of someone you miss or what they are like when they come through in dreams. People often want to know why they appear at certain ages? Why can't they appear to me all the time? Why do they seem to go away as time passes? Well, I'll try and answer some of those questions for you.

LITTLE ALLISON

When I was 6 years old, I went to my first funeral. My great-grandpa Johnson had fought a valiant battle against intestinal cancer, he finally succumbed to it. I remember seeing him lying

in his casket. I thought he was taking a nap. I didn't really understand what death was, I just knew it made people cry. It made
them sad. My mom was distraught; she really loved him. He was
a larger than life cowboy hat toting, bolo tie-wearing guy, who
was kind and funny. He was a man who was missed by many,
and he was the first apparition I ever saw. After his funeral, my
mom took me home and got me ready for bed. She tucked me in
and said goodnight. I couldn't sleep, so I peered over the edge of
my covers, thinking about the day. I looked away for a moment,
and when I looked back, I saw my great-grandfather standing at
the foot of my bed. He was smiling, looked healthy, had no lines
on his face, and sort of glowed. He said, "Tell your mom, I'm still
with her, and I'm not in pain anymore."

I was so excited, I thought he was back! So, I jumped out of
bed, ran into my mom's room, and relayed the message. She
looked less than amused, a little annoyed, and told me to "go
back to bed."

I didn't really understand why she wasn't happy to hear that he
was okay. I sulked back to my room to tell him what had happened and when I opened my door, he was gone. I was confused,
had I seen him? Did he leave? Did I not deliver his message,
right? I felt like I had done something wrong, so after that experience, I kept my sightings to myself. Even though I wasn't sure
what had happened that night, I felt relief deep inside my child's
heart. I knew that my grandpa Edward was just fine, wherever he
was.

My great-grandfather had appeared older because that's the
only way I ever knew him. He needed me to recognize him. He
had his healthy weight back, no flaws on his skin, looked vibrant

and had the kindest smile on his face. I could hear him in my heart, saying, "It's okay."

I knew he was reassuring me that he wasn't in pain, and he wasn't trapped in a box, buried six feet under. He was whole again, and his voice remained in my heart.

Sometimes, spirits appear younger because they revert to the age they were the happiest on earth. Other times, the deceased appear at an age you will recognize them like my great-grandfather did for me. Since, I'm a medium, who has no history with the dead in client readings, they show me the actual age they appear on the Otherside. They go back to the age, they were the happiest. The number they give me represents the pinnacle of their life. When the deceased fell in love, got married, had children, won a championship, whatever their version of heaven is becomes their reality.

Some people have 'visits' in dreams from their deceased loved ones. Some people see them standing in front of them. Others will just have to hear their loved one's messages relayed by people who aren't too distraught for the dead to reach. When our deceased loved ones see us hurting, it fuels them to contact us, any way, they can. They never appear frightening or sickly, like many movies and television shows portray. They look content, rested, and vibrant. When I bring them through, they make me experience the love that they feel for the person I'm reading. Their heart is filled with warm, endless love, so much of it, it could fill rooms. They show me their versions of heaven on the Otherside. The places they now reside in are emotional replicas of the landscapes that they experienced their most joyous living moments. Energy impressions of a moment exactly as it was when they made the memory. Their 'versions of heaven' are wherever and with whoever brought them joy. People who loved and lived big are easy to bring through in a reading. Our souls are constructed from the emotions and energy of our life experiences. So, the fact that I get to 'read' people's stories through readings makes me one of the world's luckiest people. They never focus on the end of their life, they live in the magic of the moments that carried the most energy. Some people ask me, "What about people who didn't truly live or love?"

It makes me sad that people who were lucky enough to be born would squander or destroy their lives. It does happen, some people are bitter, some seem almost resentful to have been born, it's a shame. It's also usually the energy they came in with, they never grew. Not, in their whole lives, did they learn from their mistakes or take responsibility for their actions. I see them as un-evolved souls, who may have to come back to change what they didn't in the last lifetime. People don't usually book readings to hear from those who dragged them down in life. Occasionally, I'll have a woman book a reading who wants to hear from her 'father.' I'm used to bringing dads through for daughters, who were "Daddy's girls." They shared such a close bond with their dad or, I'll bring a dad through who wants to apologize for not being there more for his daughter. There have been a few times that a reading took me in a darker direction. I've connected to the spirit, and all I feel is prostitutes connected to him, drinking and some-times molestation of family members. Those types of people gravitate to 'like' energy. Very rarely, but once in a blue moon, I'll connect to a spirit who isn't sorry. They lack empathy. There's something 'dark' about their energy, it's cold, almost inhuman.

People like that are never around anyone else, except others who have similar dark energy. I guess that's what we who do feel for people would consider hell.

Sometimes a person comes through and shows themselves, not smiling or with a solemn look on their face. The living often misinterprets the message. It usually depends on the circumstances around how they died. I brought a dad through for his kids and wife. I told the wife, he looked and felt sort of disgruntled. She said that her kids had both dreamt of him, and they said he looked the same way. I said, "He's not mad at them."

The deceased's son was worried because they had an argument, and his last words to his dad weren't kind. This actually happens more than people think. Listen to me when I tell you this. Petty arguments that transpired right before a person died are NOT something they hold on to, we do. We bludgeon ourselves, torment ourselves with guilt. This is not what they want. They remember the thousands of times that we told them, "I love you," The many times we hugged them and thanked them for always being there. They remember the high-fives given in celebration of a win or an accomplishment. The millions of moments that we shared feeling love for one another. We obsess over the one angry time. The one time that was the last time. We replay it, over and over again, wishing it hadn't happened.

I brought a man through once for his son. They had quarreled before his father's heart attack. His father's words to him were, "We're family, we fight and we make-up. That's what we do!"

If they can see it in that light, then can't we? Let it go. There's nothing to forgive. They always say those words, "There's nothing to forgive."

Try and really hear those words and take them to heart.

Back to the son I started with a couple of paragraphs ago. I said to his mother, "Your husband's not happy about how he died." He died doing what he loved, but in the way his wife had worried he would. His traumatic passing was her worst nightmare, and he knew it. He wasn't ready to leave his family. He wanted to take it all back.

So, yes, he's sad that his kids can't hear him, and his wife doesn't know when he's around.

I told her, "If you acknowledge that you know he wasn't ready to go, you see he wasn't happy about that at all, it will help him come to terms with his passing."

I hope my advice helped advance the family forward so they can have more uplifting dreams now. Traumatic passings that are sudden usually leave the deepest wounds. With time, the family and the man they miss more than anything they ever thought humanly possible, will find their way back to one another. They're family, the love is there, that will never change.

Sometimes the deceased has a solemn face because their family isn't acknowledging the signs they send. The family keeps explaining them away and dismissing them. There are different reasons they come through with a serious expression. It's seldom because they're mad at someone they love. There are times the deceased might be disappointed with some of your current choices. The living is usually aware of what those are and why. Please know that they don't want their death to be your source of pain or your excuse to do drugs or drink yourself to death. They want to fuel you to achieve your goals. They want to be your source of inspiration, your confidant. They want to be part of your life and for you to be part of their world too.

Many people ask me, "Why can't they stay with me all the time so that I can see them?"

Well, there's a reason why they don't appear to us all the time. Can you imagine a world where spouses never move on and complete their lives' stories because they are living in the past? Some people might say they'd prefer that, and I get it, I would probably feel that way too. The living doesn't get to make that choice. Our loved ones become part of another existence. They're powerful energy, beyond us. They're wiser, they can see farther than we can. They know what work we have left to do. If parents who lost children could see their deceased child all of the time, think of how many children wouldn't be born. We would basically already be dead because we would stop living to stay in our house with them. They disappear to force us back to life. They 'visit' so that we know they're still around us. Signs are to remind us they're okay and part of our daily lives. Signs are their heavenly bread crumbs helping us to get through the rest of our lives until we see them again.

Many people comment to me that they use to get visits in dreams regularly right after the person died, but now they don't get them anymore. After a person dies, they have a lot of energy on getting through to their loved ones. They want to let them know that they're safely on the Otherside. Once the loved one knows this, they often pull back their energy so that your life doesn't revolve around their death. This doesn't mean that they're not with us daily, they just travel in the shadows, so they can see you and know that you're getting back to living. They don't want to hold us back. You would do the same thing if you were dead.

You'd want to see your children laugh again. You'd want to see them thriving. Spouses don't like to see their mate, eating alone every night, with nothing to look forward to anymore. Grandparents watch us beaming with pride, waiting to see their strong character traits surface in their grandchildren. They see us stand up to challenges in life when others sit down. They see it when we care about others, thinking, "Grandpa would've done that too. He would've stopped to help a stranger change his tire."

Or, "Grandma would've made dinner for her neighbors knowing they're having a hard time. I should do that, too."

They see us channel their goodness. The dearly departed see us loving them through our actions. Our loved ones live inside of us, and we can show those we miss that we hear them from within.

It's true that the dead like to be talked about, fawned over, how loved and missed they are by all. The deceased love to hear funny or heartwarming childhood stories from their siblings and parents. They like to look at the pictures of themselves when they were in their prime. They like it even more when people comment on how attractive they were. They want to be thought of fondly and often. What they don't want is to derail your life. If you show them that thinking of them brings positivity into your life, you'll get more visits and more signs. If memories of them only serve to cause destruction in your life, they will be awfully disappointed. They don't want you to be reckless and blame it on their death. Put yourself in their shoes, it's an excellent way for you to know what they'd want you to do.

Debra and Sean

Debra

My 21-year-old son, Sean, lived with his grandmother in Dallas, Texas, and was doing very well. Sean was working for UPS part-time and planned to go to school to become a manager for UPS.

On May 17, 2010, I received a call that no parent wants to receive . . . that is, to hear that your child has been in a bad car accident, and it doesn't look hopeful.

My sister, Penny, kept on telling me that Sean wasn't doing well, and she was going to head to the hospital to see what was going on. It was 1:30 in the morning, Texas-time, and 12:30 a.m. in Georgia.

It took me all day to get plane tickets to get me to my son so that I could be by his side. Ryan, my oldest son, came with me, and we arrived in Texas around 9 p.m. that night. It felt like an eternity to get there. My husband, Ron, and Casey, Sean's younger brother, would arrive the next day.

As I walked into the emergency room, I couldn't believe that my son had been in a car accident and that he might not make it through the night. Ryan and I walked in the back room, and we saw Sean. He looked at peace. For someone just having had a car accident, he didn't have any significant cuts, except on his chin—but his arm and his neck were broken. The nurse told me, 'You can touch him.' And when I did, I knew he wasn't with me any longer. I didn't sense he was in his body.

My husband Ron and son Casey arrived, the whole family

stood by Sean's bed, including all of his friends. We prayed to God to watch over our son and give him peace.

We decided at that point that if Sean couldn't come back to us, and his organs were still viable, Sean would want to be an organ donor and give life to others. And that's precisely what he did.

When I came back from Dallas, I went back to work immediately, but I felt like something was pushing me to go to the book store and look at books. Something that would give me strength in my belief in the afterlife. I followed the need to go, and while I was there, I saw Allison's book, *We Are Their Heaven*, and I bought it.

This is important, because later, during my second reading, Sean had told me that he gave me, her book. This also explained why I felt like I was being prodded to buy her book. When I saw it, I felt his energy so strongly.

On March 13th, I met Allison at one of her events, and I told my sister that Sean is 'definitely here,' and he was.

That night, I was one of the audience members who received a reading, and Sean came through. He sounded so happy! He told Allison that "I'm in a good place and like the necklace that my brother wears."

The necklace had a guitar on it, and read 'RIP Sean.' He said that "I like the big picture of me, in the living room."

The picture is big, and it is Sean, sitting in front of a motorcycle, smiling. I was so relieved after the reading. But I wanted more.

So, I had a second reading with Allison.

Allison stated that she would 'bring him through,' and that it might take a few seconds. There was silence on the phone, but then she jumped right into the reading. Allison asked how long Sean had been gone, and I said it had been eleven months.

She stated that Sean and I had a solid energy binding us together.

Allison started laughing because Sean kept saying, he was the good-looking one.

Sean was taller than his older brother Ryan, and Ryan never liked being shorter. Sean had blue eyes and blond hair, he was a great-looking young man. In the reading, Sean had said "I could have been an actor or model," that's very accurate.

Sean's personality was powerful. He was the jokester amongst his friends; he could always make someone roar with laughter. Many of his friends said that the party didn't really start until Sean walked into the room. This is important because, in the reading, Sean noted that no one could believe that Sean was gone because he was the "golden boy."

Allison also said that she sees a domino effect on Sean's friends and that his death has changed them all. I do know that, because of Sean passing away, that many of them have stopped drinking, and they started turning their life around for the better.

Allison asked me if I had any questions so far, and I asked her to ask Sean what happened the night of the accident? He said, "I wasn't paying attention while driving and I tried to get out of the accident, but I couldn't fix it." He had always landed on his feet throughout his life, but was unable to correct this.

Sean thought he was invincible, and he wasn't. This was one time when even I couldn't get him out of a bad situation. This is important because I was always with Sean when he got in trouble and never left his side. It would always turn out okay, but this time it didn't.

Sean wanted me to know that I couldn't have prevented his passing. He wanted me to know that it was his time, and there was nothing I could have done to save him.

Sean explained that he was now like a counselor helping children cross over and that children like him. Children did like Sean, he would always tease them and run after them. He was a big kid.

Sean said that his cell phone is essential because he plays with it still, and it carries his energy.

His brother Casey has his cell phone. Casey wouldn't let me change Sean's number. After the reading, I asked Casey about Sean's phone, and he said, 'Yes,' he thought that something was wrong with his phone because there have been three times that Casey has gotten a missed call from Sean.

I said, "No, it's not broken; its Sean's energy."

In the reading, when Allison told me about the missed calls, it was so lovely to know that Sean was telling us that he was okay and still reaching out.

Sean said, "I still leave the refrigerator door open."

There are mornings when I wake up, and the refrigerator door is open. That's my boy!

Before I could ask Allison whom he was with, Sean explained that he was with my dad.

Sean was always very close to his granddad, so that didn't surprise me. Also, in the reading, my dad said, "I'm was sorry for the pain I had caused you, I'm very proud of you and love you."

My father died at the age of 57. He was very young, and I always felt guilty because I didn't get to say good-bye.

Sean said he was with "a man who had a lot of cancer."

That was my grandfather, who was a Baptist preacher. My grandfather said I raised a good son. The last time my grandfather saw Sean was when he was four or five years old, so it was comforting to know they were together.

Allison said, "Sean is with your grandmother on your mother's side."

I started crying. A week before the reading, my youngest sister, Rebecka, had a dream that my grandmother and Sean were together and said how "happy they were."

Rebecka was so happy to see them in the dream, and they all exchanged hugs and kisses. She said she didn't want it to end. But Sean and my grandmother told my sister to go because they were happy and content.

For me, Sean also said not to worry, because the women on my mother's side of the family love to cook, so he is eating and well taken care of. It makes me feel better knowing that they are taking care of my Sean.

The older generations on my dad's side and my mom's side loved to bake and cook, so when Sean told me that he was being taken care of, I was so happy that all my grandparents were with Sean.

Sean also talked about a picture where he was clowning around, making funny faces and rabbit ears behind a male's head. This picture was taken the week that my oldest son graduated. Sean insisted that he was "still in the family," and we know that he will always remain with us.

Sean kept showing Allison a black cat that he was playfully teasing, he said he "now took care of it."

I checked on this, and it was his girlfriend's cat. He also said that his girlfriend will never really get over him, but he really wants her to be happy again.

When I asked Allison about Sean's older brother, Sean said, "I'm worried because Ryan keeps staring at the computer, and he is very depressed. He looks at pictures of me and listens to music we both liked."

Sean and Ryan were very close; they did everything together. Ryan really doesn't know how to go on without Sean. But Sean said, "We can still hang out together, Bro!"

I have had many dreams about Sean, and in all of them, he looked about 6 years old. In the reading, Sean stated that he doesn't look 6 years old in Heaven, he's older. But that 'being little' was his best time, because he was able to be my little man.

He wanted me to take a picture out of him at that age, and remember he'll always be my little boy.

He also said that there is a picture of him holding a bat.

It was Sean's baseball picture. He later decided that he hated baseball, so I think he was trying to be funny.

Allison said, "April is significant to Sean, meaning that there is a passing or a birthday in April to somebody close to Sean."

My birthday is in April, and so is my sister, Rebecka's. Maybe not coincidentally, this reading with Allison was taking place on April 6th.

Sean also said, he wants me to hide Easter eggs, and he wants an Easter basket.

There wasn't a year that would pass where I didn't surprise my sons with Easter baskets, no matter how old they got.

Sean and his father were very close, but after Sean passed

away, Ron, had a tough time with losing Sean. Sean said to "tell Dad that he was 'the best' and that he let him get away with everything!"

He referred to a picture of Sean, Ryan, and Ron, when Sean was knee-high of Ron, and Ron had his arms around both of them. Sean said, "he felt very loved" and stated that Ron showed a lot of affection to his boys, that he never would show to anyone else. Sean always said that "My dad is brilliant; he knows a little about everything." In the reading, he reiterated that sentiment.

Sean often downloaded a lot of music, he said in the reading, that his friends are now downloading his music.

He also said, he loved his Guitar Hero, and he wanted his brother to have it.

Sean would always play that game with Casey; he loved their time together playing Guitar Hero.

Sean also pointed out that there is a picture of me kneeling down, and I'm giving him a hug, and he said, "it is the age I see him being in my dreams."

I remember that picture, and it is my Sean.

Sean loved music, and in the reading, he was playing 'Love Me Tender' from Elvis Presley. I remember my mother telling me that she and my dad would listen to 'Love Me Tender.' I think this was Sean's way of acknowledging that my dad was there with him.

When I bought Sean his first guitar, he taught himself how to play 'Stairway to Heaven.' This happened to be my favorite song, and in the reading, Allison told me, "Sean is playing 'Stairway to Heaven'."

When Sean passed away in May, it was very hard. He was

only 21 years of age. On September 2nd, Sean would have turned 22, and we blew up balloons and put notes inside of them. He said in the reading that "he got them."

He also said that he didn't like flowers, but instead to send him red balloons.

He loves the color red.

In the reading, he said, "I like American muscle cars."

Sean kept showing Allison a red car, in particular. Sean had a red Camaro. It was the car he was driving when he had his fatal accident. Allison said that "in his version of heaven, the car is fine, and he's still driving it."

Sean loved his car.

One of the most touching messages he gave was when he said, "I'm sorry that I ruined Mother's Day," and that the date of the 17th was significant.

The 17th was the day that Sean passed away. Sean kept pointing out the time he said that they "got the time wrong." I genuinely believe this, because I received a text at 3:20 am that said, "I love you, Mom." In my heart, I believe that is when Sean died.

The readings have changed my life. I feel strength and comfort, and I am not afraid to die, although I was informed by Allison that I will live a long life. I will live my life to the fullest, knowing that my son is still with me.

Sean was, and still is, my strength. We were very close, and I still feel the energy that we both have together. Sean pushed me to go to Allison DuBois's event and to pick up her book. He did this so that I would find some level of peace. I know that I will have my hard days, and there will be days when I feel like nothing ever happened. Like Sean said during the reading, "Mom, remember what you always told me? One day at a time."

My Take on Debra's Reading

I included Debra and Sean's reading in this book for a reason. Each year's energy varies. As you'll notice in the readings bringing through kids in chapter four, there's been quite a lot of perfect storms, leading to suicides and drug overdoses in the last few years. Part of this is due to the opioid epidemic, overprescribing medication, and depression. They all shared their stories to help other people through hard times and maybe even save a life or many. The mothers/aunt and their kids clearly have soulmate connections, and I thank them all for sharing their stories.

Debra and Sean's reading was much further back, and it stayed with me because of the playfulness between Debra and Sean.

Sean was a force of nature, I remember him being incredibly funny in his reading, even lighthearted. I forgot what it felt like to bring someone's child through, who didn't have a heavy heart when he died. This contrast shined a spotlight for me, on why? Why was I bringing through such a large amount of young suicides for the last several years? Well, I think that we can guess, but most people don't want to hear it or do anything about it. Some do, but we're all so overwhelmed with life; that a lot of us have mentally checked out. Technology is playing a part in people's depression.

There's too much information coming at us at all times. Younger people have to be taught to unplug, disengage from technology from time to time. They don't remember a time without it, and when they become adults, the added pressure of life becomes too much for many of them to handle. I think the concept of dying to young people has become similar to a "do-over" in a video game. Just pull the plug, right? Start over? Maybe, hope that next time the game is more fun? I really feel for young people today. When I was young, if I was stressed, I went roller skating or went to the mall and played Ms. Pac-Man. Do you remember getting lost listening to the Top 40 on the radio? Or, reading a teen magazine? Everything is so heavy now, even the stories in teen magazines.

With everyone showing us all how perfect their life is online, young people believe it's true. Gen X'ers and Boomers know a lot of them are full of ****. They show you what they want you to see, editing out the parts of their lives that are struggles or unflattering.

We have to teach young people that the high bar set online, is a facade. Reality shows aren't real, they're highly produced. Most married people on reality shows end up divorced for a reason. Young people don't have a realistic gage to show them what a somewhat normal, successful life looks like. Take your grown kids camping. Teach them how to unplug from technology. How to love themselves more than actors in a movie or a singer who uses autotune! Bring it in, get back in the zone.

The Coronavirus forced people to stay home with their families. Many people disengaged from technology because none of it matters when you're comparing it to a pandemic. Get back to basics, teach young people to meditate, listen to soft tunes, learn how to do something new, enjoy, and not care so much about what other people think. People only have power if you give it to them. Never, ever, let other people define who you are! Don't let them impose their will on you. I've been a public figure for a long time when I get an online troll talking about me as if they know me; they get blocked and deleted. People who aren't used to dealing with jerks who have no life seem to take what strangers say online personally. I had a friend Charlotte Dawson who was quite famous in Australia, she took her own life, just like the online trolls kept telling her to do. She was a model who was going to turn 47, the trolls didn't seem to think the world needed her anymore. There were other factors for Charlotte, but the online comments truly hurt her. Usually, the ugly words trolls say make them worse than anything the people they're judging did. She and I had a lengthy conversation about online trolls, consisting mostly of people who are unsatisfied with their own lives and want others to be as miserable as they are. I've never looked up a famous stranger to bother them, that just seems weird to me.

As my friend Charlotte wrestled with her own problems, some of the young people in chapter four did too. The mixture of alcohol, drugs, depression, and image issues, is a dangerous combination.

I included Debra and Sean's story so you can see and feel the difference in the energy of young people dying 10 plus years ago and young people dying now. The contrast of readings from 20 years ago, pre-9/11, before opioids, were rampant. Before people got so much attention online, was even another level of niceness. I like bringing through people, so that their loved ones can talk to them and learn how to hold that line of communication, without me. Every decade's energy has a multitude of ingredients. Let's hope that we all value what truly matters in life after this pandemic. I do believe the time parents are spending at home with their kids will be a great bonding opportunity.

I'm glad that Debra and her son made so many wonderful memories together and can continue to connect and hold on to their strong bond. Soulmates need each other, whether one is here and the other over there, or not. They refuse to let go, and there's no reason why they have to.

OLD SCHOOL

TERESA AND DAD

Teresa

Dad described himself in my reading as "funny and shrewd." Boy was he!

He said I was a "caretaker." I did a lot of caretaking for my mother, who died 6 months after him. More recently, I left my school teaching job to move and take care of my daughter's adopted baby boy, who has just made it to preschool (phew!).

Dad patted the top of his thick hair, now that he is 22 again! I found a great photo of him at age 20, still, on the quest for age 22 photo—he had a fantastic head of hair! My 'grandma's name' is Tutu, and I have been using '22' a lot as a password—Allison said to look for that, his new age popping up everywhere!

He referenced a house associated with him, wow! I inherited the family house, my dad's house, from my brother, after my brother passed. To afford to move and take care of the family baby being adopted, I would have to sell it; it pained me because it connected me to him. I was so happy to hear that it was what he wanted. He said it was okay to sell the house connected to him if it made my life easier.

Dad said to "Hold onto the memories, and let go of the stuff. Keep the photos, slides, and film." We sold his house and moved so quickly, there are still a few boxes with memories that I hadn't gotten to look at. I knew there were photos, but I was surprised to later find slides and two boxes of old home movies.

He referenced me leaning against a tall dresser, sad, and hoping they thought I had done right by them in their memorials. Allison said my dad was there when I was doing that, and he wanted me to know that all was done well, they were delighted. This was a massive relief to me! I had been leaning against that dresser two days before the reading, looking at their photos, saying, "I love you guys, I did the best I could and hope no one is mad at me. I'm going to try to call you in a few days, I hope you'll pick up."

Dad referenced "being with a son," I am assuming it is his only son, my brother, who passed in 2003, nine years after my parents. Allison said my dad was with his brother. At age 22, he and his older brother worked together on the road with a team of guys selling magazine subscriptions. It was 1932, the early years of the Great Depression. Dad had told me so many stories about that bunch of guys, the sales triumphs as well as pranks they loved to play on each other. No wonder that was his heaven!

My mother said for Allison to tell me, she was "sorry," that choked me up. Of course, she'd want to get in on a phone call, she loved phone calls! She died of stomach cancer, suffered greatly, and blamed me the whole time. I tried my best to care-take, but she was very medicated, confused, angry... and I was an easy target. She didn't have it easy growing up, as Allison said in the reading. Her father didn't pay her much attention, so she might have been a tad jealous that Dad and I were buddies. While we were still living in their house, we were visited quite a few times outside in the yard by three large white birds flying very low over us, hovering. The only place I've ever seen those birds was at the graveyard where I'd buried my family, a mile or so away. I always believed it was the family visiting me since I did-n't go to their grave as often as I should have. I buried them all together on the same day, tucking Mom and Dad's urns into my brother's coffin. Glad they liked it. Allison said that birds would be a sign from my mother that she was free from her pain. In our new home in Alaska, I've had hummingbirds come into my glassed-in porch and get trapped. I had to catch them in my hand, feeling their little hearts pounding. Then take them outside to be released.

I was trying to decide if I should book a reading with Allison (would Dad be mad that I spent money rather than trying to talk to him directly? He was such a saver!). I was walking our dog, talking to Dad about it. I passed our corner, walked the length of the street, turned around, and came back. On the snowy ground, where I hadn't noticed them the first time I'd walked by---a dollar bill and a lighter (from The Elbow Room tavern:-). Well, was Dad saying "money to burn"? We had just sold something and had a little extra cash, a little...did I just say "Elbow Room"? Dad's name was Bill, as in dollar... my daughter said, "Mom, it's so obvious." And as if to further make his point, I found a dime on the ground everywhere I went until I booked that appointment.

Ten cents was the price of a phone call when I was a teenager needing to phone home if I would be late!

Dad passed away almost 24 years ago, and I still miss him. He had congestive heart failure. My dad drove to the store and got a few groceries, so my mom could rest. He returned to his car, started the engine, put the car in reverse, and had a heart attack. His car slowly reversed and stopped when it hit a bush. An ambulance was called; Dad told Allison that he couldn't respond, but wasn't afraid, he could hear people around him. He was always a proud and independent man. I'm sure my dad didn't want to die in a bed with people hanging around staring at him. I'm sure he was happy to have some privacy, a chance to just slip off without much fuss. Allison said he hadn't wanted to be a burden.

Dad told Allison that he knew I'd said many prayers for him, and he thanked me. He had a habit of warming a bar stool on the way home from work, and I prayed every day, starting as a small school kid, that he'd make it home safely. So, my dad knew about all of the prayers, I said for him. When he did die in his car at age 83, in a 2 mph collision with a shrub. I felt God was acknowledging all of the prayers that I'd said for him throughout my life. Asking that my daddy wouldn't die in a terrible crash, I felt like Little Teresa's prayers had been answered.

MY TAKE ON TERESA'S READING

This book is a collection of stories of soulmates. I wanted to take a hard look at soulmates to better understand this powerful force that binds people together. From what I can tell from over

20 years of conducting readings, fewer people have soulmates than people who don't. Now, not all people in our lives are soulmates, but that doesn't mean they don't have a purpose in our lives. We can love someone with our whole heart without them being a soulmate. There's nothing wrong with that, they're very fulfilling relationships that we value.

Then there are those relationships in our lives that are challenging ones. Even the problematic relationships in our lives can be opportunities for spiritual growth and a way to better understand ourselves and others. We don't always know what our parents have been through in their young lives. Our youthful years are our formative years, and we carry those memories with us throughout our lives.

I brought Teresa's dad through in her reading. She was a Daddy's girl, they were very close. He was who she had hoped to hear from in the reading.

I could see why Teresa missed him, he was a character, nicknamed 'Red.' He chartered a colorful life; he had a big personality and reveled in his life in Hawaii, where he lived. He had lost his first wife to cancer before he had met Teresa's mother. He had been through a lot, watching helplessly as his first wife withered away. After her funeral, he took his daughter (Teresa's older sister) on a cruise to begin the healing process, where he met Teresa's mom. Teresa's mother was young with Hollywood good looks, but she had difficulties in her childhood that shaped her. Those formative years for her taught her how to build emotional walls. In Teresa's reading, after I brought her dad through, her mom popped in the reading. Her mother said, "I'm 19 again!" She mentioned having "nice legs now." She said, "she could wear skirts again."

She looked young, her hair looked 1940's to me, rolled back on the sides, and pinned it up. I shared how she looked with Teresa, which seemed to make her feel good, knowing that her mother had found contentment. She made some apologies to Teresa and answered some questions that Teresa had about how her mom felt about her. Teresa seemed happy to have heard from her parents for different reasons. From her dad, because she missed his presence in her life. Teresa was glad to hear from her mom because she knew that her mom now had lighter energy. She appeared at the age that she would have been thriving as a secretary at Universal Studios in Hollywood, California. Some fantastic years for her mother. Teresa later sent me pictures of her parents, a few she had discovered after our reading. She had found the slides and film reels that her dad spoke of when he came through in the reading. She was pleasantly surprised to find them, and now she can enjoy looking at the slides and film reels of her dad, that she hadn't seen before. She also sent me a picture of her mom. She was young and lively, smiling, sitting side-saddle on a parked motorcycle, wearing a skirt, with lovely legs, and her hair rolled up on the sides and pinned up. Just the way she looked in our reading. It looked like she was on the Universal set, where she spent many good days in the 1940s.

Sometimes parents make mistakes raising us because they have their own wounds. Teresa's mother had regrets about how she had treated her daughter and was able to tell her so. I hope that alleviated some of the pain Teresa carried deriving from any sour words her mother may have said to her when she was dying. When people are dying, medicated, and in pain, they sometimes say things they don't mean or wouldn't have otherwise said. Caretakers often carry guilt around feeling resentment they may have experienced, having the taxing duty of taking care of someone who was dying. The dead know that those feelings are human, and they don't take it personally. They definitely don't carry it with them to the Otherside. Their focus centers around warm memories and the love they shared with others; that's the magic in life!

Once, Teresa had her reading with me and matched my description of her mother to a picture that she found after her reading; she could see her mother in a new light. Her mother was no longer a disgruntled, dying woman, releasing her pain through words she had said to Teresa.

Teresa can now visualize her mother young and lively. Hopefully, it will help her to let go of some of the seeds of pain planted at the end of her mother's life. Teresa's mother doesn't want to hurt her daughter. She wants to be a positive presence around her.

If you had a relationship with a family member that proved frustrating and painful, from words they said to you towards their end of life. I know it's a challenging task, but don't take it personally. It's their pain talking to you. It's their fear of dying lashing out at whoever is closest to them. Forgive them their worst days and remember them on their best days. The pain and ugliness in life won't follow us to the afterlife. When you die, it's as though cool water washes over you and washes away your death and any physical or emotional wounds, you collected in life. You're restored, you become the best version of yourself. Both Teresa's parents love her; her mom just didn't know how to say it in life, but she was able to convey her love for Teresa in death.

SOUL TO SOUL

"Soulmates" is an age-old concept, dating back to ancient Greek times. Deep thinker Plato wrote about a theory that humans initially came with four arms, four legs, one head, and two faces. Zeus, King of Gods in ancient Greek religion, being intimidated by the beings, split the body in half. The separation of the two caused them to spend their lives, searching for their other half, hoping to become one, being again.

Although some people think the origin of soulmates lacks merit, this doesn't mean that Plato's idea of a soulmate, doesn't resonate with human experiences. Love is a feeling, science tries to explain it away, as no more than a chemical reaction. For many of us, we believe that love's much more than science can understand or quantify. Similarly, science has tried to weigh and measure the soul. Scientists have been unable to substantiate a soul even existing. What does that tell us? Science has some answers, but not all of them. Like my husband, Joe says, "68% of an unknown form of energy known as dark energy can't be measured, it still affects us through gravity."

Just because love and souls can't be measured by science, that doesn't mean they don't affect us, or they don't exist.

Some matters of the heart and soul, we have to figure out ourselves. Education and science are vital in the world, but we don't need science to explain everything. I was studied by scientists for four years, my readings published in academic journals. So what?

What did any of it prove? While cynics argue against life after death and believers argue for it, isn't it better for us to individually make up our minds what resonates? Deciding what feels right to each of us should help us define our understanding of something that is such a significant part of who we are, our life force, our soul.

If you talk to hospice nurses, they'll tell you that they can feel patients' souls leave their bodies when they die. Aren't they the real experts around the moment of death? Hospice nurses witnesses more people die than almost anyone else. I know souls exist because I talk to them. I have been bringing them through for loved ones every week, for the last twenty years.

Psychic/Mediums have been documented all the way back to the Egyptians' court seers, my point being that we've been around a minute or two. Even people who don't consider themselves mediums still have encounters with loved ones who die. They dream about them, talk to them, and ask for signs that they receive right away. They see them standing in front of them when they're awake. Small children talk about seeing spirits all of the time. Encountering a spirit is natural, it's so human. That's why we've all either experienced it or know someone who has dreamt of a deceased relative and interacted with them. Young adults are less likely to care because they usually haven't lost anyone who matters to them. However, some young adults fall in love, meet a soulmate, or have experienced someone in their life who "completes them."

When I press my face against my husband's chest, I can feel his 'life force.' Not just his heartbeat but all of the energy inside of him. That energy shows through in our eyes, "the windows to our soul."

You can feel love when you look into the eyes of someone who loves you, it's energy shared between you. You don't need someone with a clipboard who may have never fallen in love or had this connection with anyone, to tell you whether love and souls exist. Decide for yourselves, look deep within you, to find your truth.

People often talk about their soulmate. People who have met their soulmates have experienced a sensation like they've met this person somewhere before. Maybe even in another time. It feels like your life before the moment you laid eyes on each other never existed. It's profound, and they only feel whole when they're around that person. The bond is instant; it strengthens with time, and your need to be together grows. You feel like that place inside of you, a place you're aware exists, a space that has been searching for something, out in the world your whole life, has finally found its way home. People who don't have this void inside may be born to their soulmate, or have a child later, who fills a hole, you didn't even know you had. You didn't know that you could be so happy or fulfilled until your baby was born and looked into your eyes. Now, life without them is unimaginable.

Some flowers can live with very little sunlight. When a strong enough light breaks through the clouds, that same flower will reach towards the sky to touch the light, that it didn't know it needed. The light will make it possible for the flower to grow, to its full potential. Sometimes, children are the light we didn't know we needed. They help us to grow and feel emotions that we didn't think we were capable of experiencing. They draw out protection instincts that we didn't know we had inside of us. They fill us with a purpose that we didn't realize could dwell in our hearts.

A soulmate doesn't have to be a romantic soulmate. It can be a child, a parent, a sibling, I've heard people say a grandparent before, even a friend. When you experience a soulmate, they feel familiar to you, as though there's a deeper connection between you. It's not just a simple physical connection, it's much more. You feel like you've known them your whole life, or somehow you knew, they were coming. You might feel as though you're part of the same energy and need to be together to feel alive.

I believe that people may relive the same scenario over and over in multiple lifetimes until their soul evolves and breaks the pattern. In astrology, when your chart is run, it shows your story and your karma. In a person's chart, you can see the planets' energy behind the person's choices and what they're made of in general. Choices that could involve many lifetimes of marrying for security (money) you're now being challenged to break the cycle and make your own money, this time around. To take your power back.

Another example is, a person can live consecutive lives of hiding who they really are (could be gay and still tries to live a straight life). Maybe, this time around the timing will be right; they'll be true to themselves and own who they really are. Again, taking back their inner power.

Some people in this lifetime might be repelled by religion and not know why. In their chart, it can tell a story of them being persecuted by the church, in past lives. Helping someone to better understand their reactions and feelings. Some women don't want children in this life and don't know why. A great astrologer can see patterns in their chart. Their chart tells a story from the past that might answer the question of why.

Sometimes, experiencing a soulmate feels like you're learning a lesson that feels familiar to you. Repeating a pattern, being given a chance to choose a different outcome. Or, perhaps in a past life, the two of you were ripped apart. One of you may have died, and the other never recovered from the loss. This lifetime you get to live a long life together, have children, intertwining your lives, and ultimately dying old together. There are different relationship scenarios, but the point of your coming back together is to come full circle and wrap up unfinished business. To let the natural evolution of your souls unfold and allow you to grow together.

Hypothetically speaking, your mother may have been your sister in a past life. So you have a relationship dynamic that feels more like friends rather than mother/daughter. Some people feel like their parents act like they're the children, and they've forced their kids to assume the role of the parent. Is it possible that our soul's memory is trying to put the relationship dynamic, back the way it was, in another lifetime? Maybe, there's something that we failed to learn before.

Sometimes, we have a child, who's our soulmate. Occasionally, people have a parent that is their favorite person in the world. Other times, it's the person that you're madly in love with, the one you can't live without. A soulmate can come to us, in many forms, for a variety of reasons, but what's important is to recognize when you're lucky enough to have been graced by one.

The difference between many other people's relationships and the ones written about in this book is that the people here knew they had met their soulmate. They didn't have to ask, "If, this is their soulmate?" If you have to ask, the answers no.

You can have a nice relationship with someone you love, a fulfilling family, and be married for 50 years. Happiness can be had by all! The difference is in what I described throughout my chapters. There are plenty of people in the world who are good candidates for relationships. Maybe you could even be happy with a dozen different people, who all have qualities you're looking for in life. They check all the boxes!

A soulmate is unique, they're not perfect, you'll fight, but you know in the depths of your soul you have to be together. They're your oxygen. You're better together. When you're separated, your heart hurts, and your inner light dims.

They're the only person you will meet in this lifetime, who can send a shock through your soul, a feeling of having met before as if, you've been waiting for them your whole life. I'm always so inspired when I read a client who misses her mate, and she says, "I was lucky enough to have spent my life with my one, true love. We had passion, we had it all, and that will get me through the rest of my life until I see him again. I don't want to meet anyone else. I've had more love and happiness than I deserve. No, my memories will get me through. He's the only one for me."

There's contentment inside of them, their heart is full. The widow/widower know they were blessed to have found their other half. They have had everything they ever needed or could possibly want. I understand that feeling. I feel that way about Joe.

For everyone who came with me on my journey through my book Love Can't Tell Time, I wish you contentment and love.

What does love mean to you?

_____

_____

_____

_____

_____

_____

Write a note to someone you love.

_____

_____

_____

_____

_____

_____

_____